Shooting Hipsters

Shooting Hipsters:
Rethinking Dissent in the Age of PR

Christiana Spens

Published by Repeater Books
An imprint of Watkins Media Ltd

19–21 Cecil Court
London
WC2N 4EZ
UK

www.repeaterbooks.com
A Repeater Books paperback original 2016
1

Distributed in the United States by Random House, Inc., New York.

Cover design by Johnny Bull
Illustrations by Christiana Spens
Typography and typesetting by Jan Middendorp
Typefaces: Chaparral Pro and Absara Sans

ISBN: 978-1-910924-16-7
Ebook ISBN: 978-1-910924-17-4

Contents

For Andy and Caspian

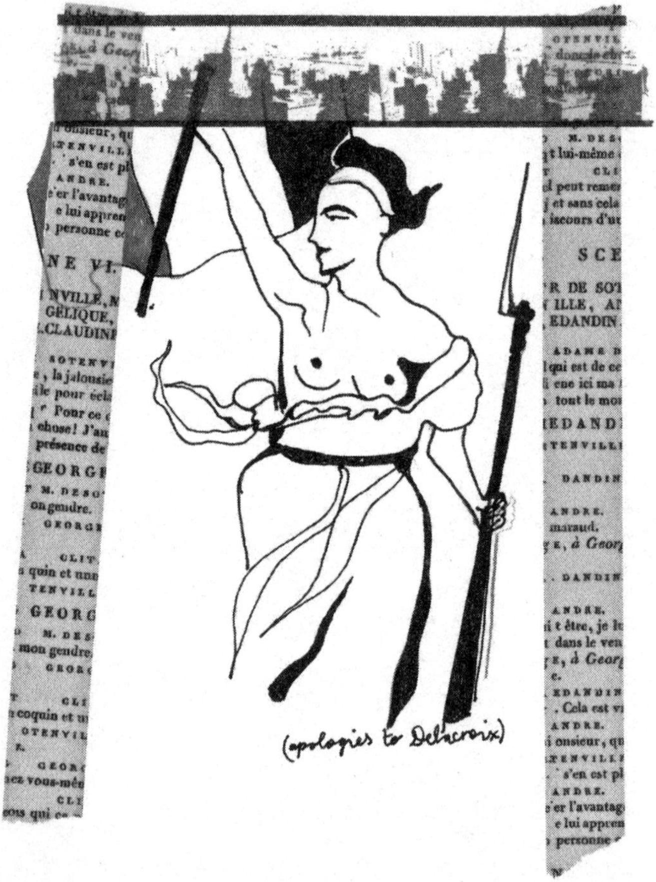
(apologies to Delacroix)

Introduction

The Romance of Dissent

Bliss was it that dawn to be alive, But to be young was very heaven! (WORDSWORTH, 1888)

Revolution, in all its manifestations, has long captured the public imagination, as well as those of artists, writers and musicians. Wordsworth wrote his famous lines not about first love, but about the French Revolution. Romanticism more generally was about revolution and anti-establishment ideals, just as much (if not more) than passionate love, Arcadian nature and the blissful sublime. The subject of sonnets, novels, songs and paintings, revolution has been glorified and admired in the arts, traditionally associated with brave young people and spectacular change.

These days, this Romantic notion of revolution is still at the core of most dissenting groups operating in the West, from the student protests against education cuts in 2010 to the Tea Party movement, and from the Provisional IRA to Al Qaeda. Anonymous has borrowed its imagery (and particularly its masks) from Alan Moore's *V for Vendetta*, itself drawing upon tales of an attempted revolution past and Guy Fawkes' part in it, while the Occupy movement has been supported by a vast array of creative projects, from rousing rhetoric to books of writings inspired by the movement. Occupy have also turned vacant buildings into pop-up libraries and created political spaces such as the Bank of Ideas in London, as well as making digital films, comic books and 'subvertisements'. It is difficult, in fact, to imagine revolution without art, or at least this notion of a Romantic spirit that persists through the centuries.

Dissent is often necessarily public: the point of so much civil resistance is to communicate a message, whether that is through 'propaganda of the deed' – an idea attributed to Russian anarchists in the 19th century, and the foundation of modern 'terrorism' – or through protest songs and literature. Where the French Revolution had Wordsworth and Delacroix, we have CNN and photos in the tabloids. The French Revolution also sparked its fair share of anti-revolutionary propaganda, in England particularly, such as Edmund Burke's *Reflections on the Revolution,* but over time the image of revolution from the Romantics has persisted more than such opposing views of the era. It is of course too early to know how the dissent of our time will appear in the history books; it could be that the subversive voices in art and literature become better known with time. At the moment, however, the very powerful mainstream media seem to lower these voices to a faint whisper, with sensationalism and the politics of anxiety. One thing is true though, whether it is effective these days or not: dissent has a long tradition of courting the public through media and art.

The media and artists benefit from this relationship. Wordsworth got a poem, Delacroix a masterpiece now housed in the Louvre – and CNN gets ratings. When a terrorist attack happens, everybody watches the news and scrolls through photographs online; people watch with fascination, outrage and sadness – but importantly, they watch. The attacks on the Twin Towers in New York during 9/11 were astonishing because, as was oft-repeated at the time and since, "it was like a film." And this was no accident: the members of Al Qaeda who hijacked the plans made sure that there would be a time lapse between the two attacks, so that the press would be assembled for the second attack, for maximum exposure. People learned of the attacks through the same loop of footage on every channel, repeating over and over in playback. It was impossible for ordinary people to escape from, attached as Western civilians are to their televisions, no matter how far people were from the action.

"If it bleeds, it leads," as the old adage goes; and even non-violent dissent can cause a spectacle that people fixate upon. These themes and feelings that captured the minds of the Romantic poets – rebellion, pride, excitement, ecstasy – continue to draw new audiences, and new protesters. But these days it is the news channels and the tabloids that are reaping the rewards. The Romantics and the revolutionaries won their battle in a symbolic sense at least; but overwhelmingly, in recent years, those various anti-establishment groups who protest or fight the status quo have not won theirs.

The education cuts and rise in tuition fees still happened. Northern Ireland is still in the United Kingdom, even if inequalities between Catholics and Protestants are less so and the British Army is no longer patrolling the streets. A Peace Process and a compromising seat in government is usually the best that a revolutionary group can hope for these days. Being damned as 'terrorists' and locked in Guantanamo are among the worst. The demands of dissenters are rarely granted, whatever their cause, although the desires of the tabloids are routinely accomplished. The traditional assumption has been that publicity is always beneficial to dissenters. But it is simply not true that, as Oscar Wilde once quipped: "The only thing worse than being talked about is not being talked about."

Why is this? Why do highly publicised protests and dissent have little political effect, or only a damaging one, in spite of their media attention? For a start, sensationalistic press tends to focus on violence and punishment rather than politics, making non-violent and legal dissent difficult to publicise. This, combined with an over-reliance of dissenting groups on tactics of public protest and disruption, makes groups vulnerable to infiltration, sabotage and the unpredictable behaviour of rogue dissenters. Violence is usually bad PR for a dissenting group, even if it can attract attention to the cause – it is not the right kind of attention, and tends to result in the dissenting group being termed 'terrorist' or 'criminal', rather than a legitimate political protest. Violence is very easily framed by the media as a moral failing, especially if that violence is against civilians or property. Even when a group is not violent, the media and authorities tend to conflate these two kinds of civil resistance (legal and illegal), which is potentially undermining for legal and peaceful groups, whose image will be tarnished.

If the current political spectrum has been pushed to the right, if the Overton Window (or the range of ideas the public will support) is biased towards the right, then anything remotely left-wing will be depicted as impossibly radical. Normal, reasonable things that used to be everyday and taken for granted (public ownership of railways and electricity for example) are painted as unthinkable, and unthinkable things (bank bailouts and bonuses, participation in foreign wars and so on) are painted as reasonable.

The reason that these issues are really problematic for dissenting groups, however, is that many of the groups themselves are naïve about their relationship with PR and the media, as well as overly dependent on tactics such as public protest. This book will explain why certain PR strategies work better than others, finding that sometimes avoiding publicity and using tactics other than protest is the best form of political action to take. Relying on the mainstream media to accurately represent a group's actions and ideas is naïve.

How political groups and their causes appear to the public is of course a major factor in their success, particularly in an age where the media is so present in people's lives, but it is not the only thing that should be considered here. What lies behind that appearance obviously matters just as much, and generally more so. Sometimes appearances are quite representative of who a person or group are and what they are trying to do. At other times, appearances can be deceptive – sometimes to the benefit of a political actor, and sometimes to their detriment. When it comes to anti-establishment groups, there is a tendency for mainstream media to represent their identity and views in a way that is unflattering, especially if those views oppose elements of the establishment, or views they share. And yet negative PR can affect those in the established political parties as well; it is a part of being in a democracy that the press may take issue, however fairly or unfairly, with those in power as well as those aspiring to it. It is, if anything, the press' *raison d'être* that it should take issue with those in power, being as it were the 'fourth estate'. In 1787, Edmund Burke said in Parliament that there were "Three estates in Parliament; but, in the Reporters' Gallery yonder, there sat a Fourth Estate more important far than they all." They are, then, there to hold power to account, but also (in doing so) exerting a power themselves (Schultz, J. 1998, 49).

This book is concerned with the ways that this powerful media represent anti-establishment groups, rather than politicians or causes in the mainstream. It is also focused on the ways that groups are depicted in the press in the West, particularly the UK and the US, within a democratic context. The range of groups looked at is wide, though, in their attitudes to the law and to violence, in their place on the political spectrum, and in their loyalty to the principles of democracy. This is not because I think of them as similar (evidently, Occupy and ISIS have very little in common), but because they all have quite different attitudes to PR, and have been treated differently by the press for those reasons and others. By 'dissenting groups', therefore, I simply mean that these groups are anti-establishment, and dissent from mainstream politics.

There are complications involved in taking this approach, and in referring to such different groups and causes in one discussion. Whatever a group's PR strategy, some groups will have inherently more sympathetic or compelling causes and points than others, so the media, and those who decide who to report on and how, will inevitably treat a group they consider dangerous and immoral quite differently to one that seems fair and legitimate, particularly if the publication or TV channel in question shares those principles. That said, the media organisations in question also want ratings and stories, so even if a group is dangerous and threatening, or rather, especially if it is, then they may cover its attention-seeking stunts because it is in the public's interest to know, and because it is, quite simply, a good story. It is not true that all publicity is good publicity of course; the media can report on a group in such a way that they win little or no support, and in fact alienate many people.

So dissenting groups, or anti-establishment groups broadly speaking, need to think about their relationship to PR in this context. If they are being reported on negatively in the press it may be because the press have different values, or are defined by another ideology. It may be that they genuinely consider those groups and individuals dangerous and divisive. These reasons for negative portrayal are worth paying attention to rather than dismissing. While a dissenting group need not define itself according to what the press says about it, it may be worth paying attention if what it does in the public eye alienates people; maybe it means that its ideas or actions are unpalatable to a lot of people, as much as it means that they have been reported on in an unflattering way. Maybe that group needs to think about how (and whether) it can appeal to a wider audience, and if it cannot, then what is its point? Is it enough simply to record discontent or to start a discussion?

These are not easy issues to consider, and can lead to political disillusionment, certainly. But reflection on these matters can also help improve not only how a group (or person) communicates with the public, but also its central principles. It is a difficult balance to make, but if a group does want to appeal to a lot of people, as most political groups do when operating in a democracy, then it does need to think about its relationship with the mainstream press, with the public who read and watch current events through that medium, and whether or not their ideas are truly compatible. If they are not, then how does an anti-establishment group proceed in a way that will actually be effective? It is easy enough to be destructive, but even the most spectacular political violence often has very little long-term effect, other than to serve as a useful narrative of evil for those already in power.

By 'Dissenters' I mean simply a qualified description rather than a group in any meaningful sense; the political groups mentioned are placed together (and discussed) according to their PR strategy and their sharing some level of anti-establishment principle. The overriding interest or point of the book is to understand the relationship between the media and anti-establishment groups, and how and why some groups succeed while others do not. PR is only one part of why a group does well or badly in achieving its goals, but it is a significant issue and one that is often overlooked or ignored, or conversely used as the only reason for a group's failure. If a group does succeed, it is likely a combination of its principles and ideas being workable and compelling to a large number of people, and its public image communicating those ideas well. If a group does badly, it could be the failure of one or the other, or both. This book is concerned with the PR side of things and does not discuss the pros and cons of particular ideas, only how they are communicated and how even good ideas can be undermined by bad press. PR can make an otherwise strong movement seem ridiculous, violent, or comic; it can make thoughtful people seem absurd, and intelligent voices go unheard, just as it can give excessive attention to destruction and mayhem or empty rhetoric. A group working within a media-saturated democracy cannot ignore that fact, just as it cannot be delusional about fighting for political ideas few people are likely to support if it wants to be successful.

The aim of this book, then, is to find out which PR tactics are best used, and which are best avoided. By examining a range of groups through the prism of their PR strategies (or lack thereof), *Shooting Hipsters* will find out which approaches work the best, discussing the pros and cons of using violence or being associated with it, the utilisation of grassroots media (including local and counter-cultural media) by populist groups, and the shunning of publicity altogether by clandestine figures and organisations. Clearly there will be no single PR strategy that fits all groups, but the aim nevertheless is to consider a range of options and discuss the situations in which some decisions work better than others when it comes to dealing with the media and publicising one's cause.

Relating to the public is central to all politics, in a democratic society especially, but 'public relations' can nevertheless seem obscure to many people and groups. If a dissenting group operating in an age where PR is so central is to succeed, however, it must face the reality of it, rather than falling victim to a complex network influenced by business interests, ideological bias of large news organisations, and old-fashioned sabotage by political enemies. *Shooting Hipsters* will assist in that reality check, without being biased towards or focused on any particular group; rather it is interested in how groups (keeping to the US and the UK) relate to the media, how the public are communicated to by political actors (whether in the establishment or against it), and how PR can so easily confuse issues and people.

In order to do so, I will first of all discuss the context of the modern focus on PR by looking at the historical relationship between dissenting groups and their political action, and the media. In **Protest and the Media: A Brief History**, this complicated, even symbiotic relationship will be examined, considering the nature of propaganda and its connection to violence, and how politics, violence, communication and the public interact.

The second chapter, **Oxygen for Terrorists**, will question specifically the traditional assumption that publicity is always beneficial to dissenters, setting up for the central discussion about why it sometimes is not, when it is, and what this means for other groups, then and now. Looking at the case of the British government and press attitudes to the IRA in the 1980s, and the way in which the hunger strikes and death of Bobby Sands changed the conversation, the chapter will consider how no publicity and bad publicity can be turned around.

In chapter three, **The Business of Bad Publicity**, I look at the ways in which big business and mainstream politics influence media and dissent, and crucially their relationships with one another. Whether making money, winning seats in government or gaining awareness of a political cause, this network of power and influence ultimately depends on an audience watching (and then voting and buying), which leads to a discussion on the nature of that political theatre, and how and why it works.

In the fourth chapter, **The Political Spectacle**, ideas about the theatre of political dissent and the media are looked at in more depth, so that the notion of public relations can be understood in that context. The nature and reasons behind the portrayal of politicians and protesters as heroes and villains will be explored, including ideas about voyeurism, violence, and the sublime.

Chapter five, **The Stylish Kids in the Riot**, looks at political movements that have relied on public protest and fallen victim to bad press, particularly coverage which depicts protesters as frivolous and idiotic, so discrediting the cause. Cases such as the 2010 anti-austerity protests in London will be examined, and in particular the way in which the protests were condemned by the mainstream media, and draconian punishments presented as justified. Dissent was not only trivialised in this case, but also reprimanded, and the movement was therefore damaged, being seen by many as illegitimate on account of this public image. While all publicity might be good publicity for those chasing fame, it is not true of groups who want to affect political change.

In chapter six, **Popular Dissent**, the book turns to populist movements such as the Tea Party movement, Occupy, Stop the War and others who relied on community support and mainstream media coverage of their protests and political arguments. Though very different politically, Occupy and the Tea Party movement have relied on similar PR techniques, to varying success.

In chapter seven, **Narcissists with Bombs**, I look at political violence that is especially exhibitionist (such as the murder of Lee Rigby and the Boston Bombs) to the point of being devoid of real political substance, and discuss this phenomenon's effect on the perception of political dissent generally, and violent dissent especially.

Chapter eight, **Shock and Awe: Performativity, Machismo and ISIS**, discusses the PR strategy of ISIS, and how the group's use of extreme violence relates to a 'war of images' and 'war of masculinities' with the US and UK, and is therefore a form of warfare in itself. I will discuss whether or not violence ever works (from a PR point of view) and conclude that more often than not, violence undermines a political cause in the long term.

Chapter nine, **Clandestine Dissent**, considers the alternative to seeking maximum publicity for a cause, and the inherent benefits of covert dissent – to the movement as well as its image. Clandestine groups such as Anonymous and WikiLeaks, for instance, have been far more successful than groups that rely on public violence or protest. The former groups have the advantage of seeming 'legitimate' in some sense to many people, rather than clearly criminal, as violent groups discussed in previous sections often come across.

In chapter ten, **Turning the Camera**, I look at scandals in which images and other data were leaked, such as Abu Ghraib as well as instances of investigative journalism that have exposed injustice and crime on the part of the state or big corporations, and the political effects therein. The idea of political critique rather than dissent *per se* is considered as an alternative to dissent that relies on PR in the ways discussed previously, including the ways in which art, literature and music can be means of dissent as well as a way of observing it.

In the last chapter, **Beyond Martyrs and Terrorists**, the findings of the previous chapters are discussed further, especially their main conclusions – namely that violence and other illegal behaviour often gets publicity, but usually doesn't help the cause, and is usually unsustainable long-term; that non-violent civil resistance has been shown to be more effective than violent, but it can be hard to get publicity, so must be managed well; and that while the Internet can be useful for some groups, it is best seen as one tool of several. It is necessary to understand the risks involved in over-reliance on the Internet. Another important finding is that using PR to focus on the issues that a group is concerned with (such as through investigative journalism), rather than the group's image, works particularly well. Art, music and literature, furthermore, are often overlooked as means of dissent but have proven uniquely valuable over the years as means of protest as well as forms of more detached (or philosophical) critique and contemplation about the issues dissenting groups are concerned with, as well as dissent itself.

Of course different dissenting groups will have particular PR strategies, according to their own principles and aims, but overall, these points will help most groups become more sustainable through an awareness of public relations, based on related cases. The murder of Lee Rigby was a clear example of what not to do, given its immediate condemnation in the press and alienating effect on the public; elements of the Tea Party movement's strategy, along with successful populist groups such as Stop the War and Occupy, although not completely successful, show the specific measures that have worked to their benefit and can be applied elsewhere. Covert measures as used by Snowden, WikiLeaks and Anonymous have worked in the short term, but have provoked great repression from above because they employ illegal action, which has probably had a negative effect on other dissenting groups (although, conversely, their findings have inspired many to fight for civil liberties and be aware of state repression and surveillance).

Overall, dissenting groups tend to be depicted as reckless, extreme and impulsive or irrational, to varying degrees, according to their behaviour but also an existing stereotype of dissent as illegitimate and possessing 'Romantic' qualities (at best), and criminal, threatening qualities (at worst). Compounding this image is the attraction to drama and spectacle that exists within the media (and the public), which will usually be captivated by violence and heightened emotions over serious political action, and therefore favour the melodrama of reckless subversion rather than sincere and non-violent civil resistance.

I conclude by elaborating on these findings and comparisons, and speculating on what can be done to redefine dissent and utilise the democratic right to protest in a culture where the trivialisation of dissent can sell magazines and undermine anti-establishment political thought. When handling the media, careful risk management is key, especially with regard to publicity. A clear and long-term PR strategy and plan to manage the media makes sense, including the use of tactics aside from demonstrations and an over-reliance on publicity; and the avoidance of violence, and disassociation with violent factions, as this is not good publicity in the long term. Political actors will usually find that it is in their best interests to influence the media where possible, to help define the narrative, or counter a dominant one. Propaganda goes both ways.

Dissenting groups can use the media to their advantage, through telling the public of their grievances, repression and injustices, which will strengthen the cause and its popularity. If the mainstream media seems to have no interest in representing dissenting groups accurately or sympathetically, meanwhile, local media may do, as well as counter-cultural publications and art more generally. A movement that is embraced by its own community, whether local, cultural or political, is likely to be more sustainable than one that is not. Either a very careful and adaptive campaign that makes better use of new media, the counter-culture and local media, or the use of other tactics of non-violent dissent, are the best options for a dissenting group to take.

By knowing legal rights, having legal representation on hand, and keeping good relations with the authorities where possible, a dissenting group has a far better chance of affecting political change and being sustainable. It is important to remember that dissent, when legal, is a democratic right, not a crime. An asserted effort must be made to sustain that democratic right, in the face of reforms that may effectively criminalise it. This is perhaps the most important point: if a group's aims are democratic in essence, then the awareness of undemocratic reforms and punishment is key. Any democratically orientated dissenting group should campaign against undemocratic reforms even if it is not their main political focus, for their own sustainability and legal right to function. The main threat to dissent is undemocratic criminalisation of that dissent. Dissent can, however, adapt to even undemocratic and unfair repression, and repression can alienate the people that the (democratic) governments depend on for power. The question for these governments is whether they want their own people to become 'the enemy', or whether it's a better idea to compromise with their demands, when democratically presented. This is why going the non-violent, legal route is best for dissenting groups in the long term; it is the best shot at true change, with the eventual support of the population, the community and ultimately the government that is meant to represent them. Once these civil liberties are secured (and this is a constant task), changing the way we tell stories and publically protest is how we can move beyond the simplistic political circus that dissenting groups inevitably get caught in.

While the Romantic spirit will persist with new ideas and rebellions, its apparent incompatibility with the mainstream news media means that it must find new outlets and tactics. Until the heads of tabloids have the visions of Wordsworth, Shelley and Byron, revolutionary dissenters will have to find new ways to glorify their causes, and communicate their ideas to the people.

Although Romanticism is all very well, it needs to be backed up by *realpolitik*. Idealism needs to be followed by action – by pragmatic ideas that will change society for the better. That is what really keeps people on side – not a passing desire or charming idea or even a charismatic speaker. Permanence is key: a movement needs to persist beyond its flurry of idealism and fifteen minutes of fame (if it gets that far). While PR is always important for anyone in politics, not least those who want to change the status quo, it is but one tactic in winning attention and approval from the public. A good public image must be accompanied by substance and well thought-out plans to make those ideals a reality. Likewise, good ideas and plans for a better world will fall flat if they are not communicated well to the public. PR and politics are about winning people over, but they are also about keeping their support. The central requirement of PR here is that it shows a group in a good light, and that it communicates genuinely good ideas and strategies that will not only compel people initially but also win their support for months and years thereafter. That means that the *realpolitik* has to be as persuasive as the rhetoric.

With that in mind, a brief history of dalliances between various dissenting groups and the public follows. In some cases, that first spark (sometimes literally) has led to movements that grew and lasted. Quite a lot of the time, though, a political group's time in the public eye was over as quickly as it began. People's attention may be easy to gain for a short time; but the public are hard to woo and keep for longer, fickle as they are.

Rolling 24-hour news with short bursts of drama has created short attention spans; current events seem to change so rapidly and reverberate so noisily that there is less sense of evolution or stability or reason. Although the Internet has been empowering to people in the sense that they can comment on articles and feel involved, there is on parallel a feeling of being overwhelmed and made impotent by the sheer mass of information and events, and a lack of certainty as to what has really happened, and what is really most important. Politicians in power (such as Osborne, clasping austerity measures, for instance) then know how to pick an opportune moment of mass panic and perceived instability to offer a policy or message that promises security (often literal as well as emotional). In this moment, his ideas appeal to a ravaged public because they contrast sharply with the so-called chaos of the world; he appears firm, resolute and even heroic in his simple meanness. So dissent, however peaceful (but better if it is violent, for these purposes), can always be turned around to benefit the establishment, and those with otherwise unpopular policies to pass through. Dissenting groups, when dismissed by the establishment and media, may do well therefore to emphasise their public support for reasonable policies or demands, rather than fall into the trap, set again and again, of becoming one more story of chaos and disorder with which to present a seemingly attractive set of opposing ideas, no matter the reality behind their spin. The political establishment has been dealing with dissent and the media for some time now, and they have learnt their lessons. Many dissenting groups, it would seem, have not.

Chapter One

Protest and the Media:
A Brief History

Political violence and protest have always had a complicated, even symbiotic relationship with the media. The media depends on unrest for stories and ratings, because people find it interesting and even entertaining; for dissenting groups, the media is seen as necessary to get the message across to a wider audience. This is part of a long, complicated relationship between anti-establishment groups, the media, and the establishment itself, that goes back to the Russian Anarchists' use of 'propaganda of the deed' in the 19th century. *Narodnaya Volya* (*The People's Will*) was a left-wing group operating in several Russian cities at the end of the 19th century, which campaigned for universal suffrage, freedom of press, communal self-government, and the transfer of land to the people, among other things. After a campaign of 'regular' propaganda, such as distribution of their newspapers, *The Worker's Gazette* and *Narodnaya Volya*, the group turned to more radical means of communicating their message and enforcing political change. After seven attempts, the group assassinated Tsar Alexander II on Sunday the 13th of March 1881 on the streets of St. Petersburg, when 20 year-old Nikolai Rysakov threw a bomb at his carriage. The Tsar was immediately taken to the Winter Palace where he was given Communion and died later that day of his extensive and terrible injuries.

Through this violent stunt, *Narodnaya Volya* had communicated their message of revolution not only to the immediate target and the state, but to the public, through the recently invented newspapers. People were apparently more interested in reading about politics via a violent attack than through regular polemics. Nevertheless, the people did not support *Narodnaya Volya* to the extent that the group really made any progress politically in the way they had envisioned. Their violence certainly made them famous, but it did not give them their demands. The Russian government, meanwhile, launched a counter-offensive, ultimately exiling, killing or imprisoning the group's members.

Despite the fate of *Narodnaya Volya*, though, their tactic of 'propaganda of the deed' became popular with other dissenting groups, especially as the media developed. After the invention of the printing press in 1830 came pamphlets and news stories about anarchism and rebellion; with satellites and TV (from 1968) came longer dramas involving plane hijackings, in which the TV channels would play a part in the drama themselves, by interviewing hostages or terrorist groups, and by exploiting the panic of families and onlookers. The Popular Front for the Liberation of Palestinian People (PFLP) favoured plane hijackings. Their first was El Al Flight 426, which, en route from London Heathrow to Leonardo da Vinci-Fiumicino Airport and then Lod Airport, was redirected to Algiers. One of three PFLP members on board knocked out the co-pilot with his pistol and ordered the pilot to fly to their new destination, while the two other members kept passengers in a state of terror, wielding hand grenades and pistols. At Dar El Beida airport non-Israeli passengers were let off, while the hijackers kept twelve Israeli passengers and the plane crew hostages – eventually letting them go after negotiations with the Israeli and Algerian governments, in a prisoner exchange. After this initial success, the group continued to hijack planes (to varying degrees of success, but usually maximum publicity, either way), as did further groups with prisoners to free and agendas to publicise. Television and satellite – newly invented – meant that these dramatic stories would usually find an audience. Hijackings were invented to exploit this new public interest and ability to watch as well as read.

With the invention of the Internet and the popularity of social media, groups such as ISIS have adapted once again, for example by putting violent acts such as beheadings and torture, or speeches filled with threats and bravado, on YouTube, and recruiting teenagers via Twitter. As the audience has become more involved in the media, conveying a message has become at times more intimate and direct, and recruitment more global and disparate.

What is contemporarily known as 'terrorism', then, is an inherently attention-seeking tactic that evolved from 'propaganda of the deed'. It communicates a political message to its audience through spectacular violence. Recent terrorist events such as the Moscow theatre siege and 9/11 were clearly designed with the global audience in mind. While the Moscow attack was actually in a theatre, the 9/11 attacks resembled, as many said at the time, some terrifying Hollywood thriller. Those attacks, without the media, would not have been designed as they were, let alone have had the huge global impact they did. Other terrorist attacks such as the murder of Lee Rigby, the Boston Bombings, and ISIS's filmed beheadings were likewise dramatic stunts that aimed to draw as much attention as possible to the perpetrators' cause, to tempt the state (or states) into overreaction, and to influence public opinion and put pressure on them to change various foreign or domestic policies (existing or subsequent) that they considered unjust. Whether terrorism works or not (and when, if so, it does) is a subject for another book, but as a PR move it has the effect, at least, of drawing attention. As we'll discuss later, however, this may not ultimately get a movement very far, whether it's extreme violence such as ISIS's filmed beheadings, or much less fatal or dangerous violence such as vandalism at a protest. A message can be seen and heard by millions and have less than desired reactions. It is an unpredictable tactic, to put it mildly.

But propaganda of the deed is not only about drawing attention to a cause. Iconoclasm for example (recently and in the distant past) is also a kind of propaganda of the deed. Designed to shock, upset and scare, violence against buildings and art undermines the messages and identity of existing political ideologies and groups as well as asserting the dominance of the iconoclasts and their contrasting belief system. During the Reformation in the 17th century, for example, Puritans destroyed Catholic art and cathedrals; later on, in the early 20th century, the Suffragettes damaged artworks held by public galleries, as "property that belonged to the nation" (Mohamed in Barber & Boldrick (eds.), 2013, 115). The attack was on the public space of the gallery or museum as much as the artwork, though; the space represented the people and the state in virtue of its accessibility and funding channels. The attack would also (and crucially) be seen; an audience and a public interest were a given. When Mary Ricardson attacked Diego Velázquez's renowned painting, *The Rokeby Venus*, with a meat cleaver on March 10th 1914, for example, she exclaimed, as she was publicly arrested and removed by police: "Yes, I am a Suffragette. You can get another picture but you cannot get another life, as they are killing Mrs Pankhurst" (qtd. in Gell, 1998, 62-5).

More recently, ISIS shattered ancient cities in Syria and Iraq, and their prized art and monuments, including artefacts in Iraq's Mosul Museum (the attacks there were also filmed). These deeds tend not to kill, but through dramatic action they state the new ideologies they represent and convey. A war of symbolism and imagery is inherent in these assaults, dubbed 'heritage terror' by some, including Dr Stephennie Mulder: "This is a propaganda video that is intended as an act of heritage terror. [ISIS] know this kind of action will cause alarm in the international community... It demonstrates their mastery over everything. Their mastery over the past and it has a deep impact on the people of Iraq as well as [those] who cherish these objects" (Mulder, 2015).

A deed need not even be violent to have a similar effect, however, and to have a similar relationship with the media and the public. The past century's public protests in the UK and US are also related to the idea of propaganda of the deed. A protest – a march, with placards, chants and slogans – is a dramatic action intended to communicate a message in a rebellious way (even when entirely peaceful). The action aims to put political ideas centre stage – to win a part in the wider political spectacle and therefore to achieve attention for the cause. It is a publicity stunt, and therefore a form of propaganda of the deed just like violent acts dubbed 'terrorism' or iconoclasm. Protest probably relies on the media more than terrorism and iconoclasm, because the deed itself is not generally as shocking or permanent. A march is transient, placards are discarded and slogans forgotten far more so than a collapsed building, broken masterpiece, or ruined lives. Protest, to have any effect, usually needs to be recorded. (Of course terrorism and iconoclasm also tend to draw in the press.)

It is not my intention to conflate violent 'terrorist' groups such as ISIS with non-violent and legal dissenting groups, but to understand the latter in that wider context of dissent and public relations. Given that legal groups are often lumped into the same category as violent groups by the media, to some extent, which in itself is a substantial problem for peaceful, legal groups, it follows that if we are to understand how dissenting groups should use PR to their advantage, we need to know how other groups use it. They are relevant associations, if not welcome ones.

One group can learn from another, furthermore: a legal group that is against austerity measures, for instance, can learn from ISIS's grasp of social media and video-editing skills. They can also observe that the use of horrific violence by that same group, while appealing to some of their supporters, alienates many people, and that the use of violence more generally may therefore be a mistake for their own political movement. In essence, by discussing a wide range of groups and a broad spectrum of dissenters, and their use of various PR strategies, we can learn and apply those findings to (ideally) democratic and peaceful groups.

The relation of dissent to violence and violence to politics will also be discussed, given its relevance to this subject, and the underlying question of why the media covers some political statements and groups, and not others, and why the public engages with some politics and not others. The conclusions from those discussions will inform the ultimate question of how a dissenting group should conduct itself in a world so influenced by PR, performance and appearances, and how the public should engage with all political actors when they are inevitably treated as an audience.

Chapter Two

Oxygen for Terrorists

Dissent is and always has been entwined with media depictions of it, whether it wants to be or not, and whether that coverage is beneficial or not. The traditional assumption is often that it is, however; as Thatcher famously announced: "We must try to find ways to starve the terrorist and the hijacker of the oxygen of publicity on which they depend" (Moseley, 1985). Thatcher's government used censorship against the threat of the Provisional IRA in the 1980s, as well as the ANC, who were at the time branded 'terrorists' also (and Nelson Mandela in particular). The voices of Irish Republicans were dubbed with the voices of anonymous actors, in a bizarre and at times comic form of censorship, which bore more resemblance to a Monty Python sketch than anything else. (*The Day Today* in fact aired a sketch, 'IRA Bomb Dogs', in which terrorists were seen speaking having sucked helium.) The British press, meanwhile, whenever it did mention the IRA, did so with dehumanising and insulting language. The *Times* (20/09/90) described the IRA as "gloating" and quoted Thatcher as calling the IRA "cowardly... wicked and evil" and their actions that of "depravity." *Punch* magazine has at various times compared the Irish revolutionaries (the IRA of the 1920s as well as post-1960s) and the Irish more generally to chimps, Frankenstein, crazy drunks, pigs, a vampire, an inferno, Jekyll and Hyde, and various images of idiocy and barbarianism. In 'The Irish Frankenstein', for example, the caricatured representative of the Irish people wears a hat with horns sticking out, ripped trousers and coat and broken shoes. He brandishes a club at a well-dressed man in a top hat, and stands with his legs splayed and a pipe sticking out of his lips, eyes wild and beard unkempt. In 'The British Lion and The Irish Monkey', meanwhile, the caption reads: "One of us MUST be 'Put Down'" – under a picture of an irate monkey with menacing teeth and clawed hands, opposite a stately and grand lion, his demeanour proud but demure.

In general, however, (aside from provocative cartoons) the Provisional IRA was given as little coverage as possible from the 1970s onwards, in line with Thatcher's insistence that depriving the cause of any publicity would stifle them. Indeed it did, but the Provisional IRA fought back with actions that would win their cause and people worldwide interest and at times solidarity, if not from the British press (who only changed tack in the 1990s, after the peace talks). The Hunger Strikes, and specifically the death of Bobby Sands, offered a narrative that went some way to counter the British press' dismissal of the Republican cause.

The hunger strikes (there were ten deaths in all from the strikes – Sands' was the best known) took place in Long Kesh prison in Belfast, at the end of a long protest. The disagreement that triggered the protest regarded prisoner status: the Republican prisoners (eight were Provisional IRA, and two were INLA – a more socialist break-off from the Provisional IRA) wanted to be recognised as prisoners of war, while the Thatcher-led government insisted that they be treated as non-political criminals.

While the 'dirty protests' began as a long campaign of non-cooperation, continued mistreatment by prison guards and a refusal to take their arguments seriously by the Thatcher-led government meant that these protests evolved into the hunger strikes. These began in 1980 and ended in October 1981. Although technically non-violent, obviously the hunger strikes involved casualties – deaths of the strikers themselves, and then related violence in the form of retributory killing of prison officers. Nevertheless, they went some way to change the public image of the Republican movement from violent perpetrators and troublemakers, to tragic victims. These acts of self-sacrifice "gained unprecedented legitimacy for the nationalist cause" (Fierke, 2014, 107). From a public-relations perspective, the hunger strikes were successful, although clearly at a terrible cost to human life. Drawing on familiar pacifist and religious iconography (Feldman, 1991, 220; Fierke, 2014, 111), popular support for the hunger strikers, the other prisoners, and the Republican cause itself rose exponentially as a result. The use of Catholic symbols and ideas such as, most obviously, a crucified Jesus and the act of martyrdom, were especially significant in attracting attention, sympathy, and a sense of camaraderie with the strikers. Pamphlets made these connections explicit, too: one put an image of Christ on the cross next to a photograph of one of the strikers, the caption reading: "He too was a prisoner of conscience" (English, 2003, 210; Fierke, 2014, 111). Being socialised into religion, and a religious way of thinking – having these themes and ideas indoctrinated into one's thoughts – meant that martyrdom as an idea was already normalised in the people of Ireland. Public rituals of self-sacrifice, and symbolic gestures about life, death and resurrection, were inherent in the hunger strikes, and meant that these protests chimed with the people on a deep level. These stunts used ideas and rituals that mattered to people, that touched them on an emotional and even spiritual level, and therefore connected these political activists with the grandest religious ideas. They asserted a sense of identity that was bound up in Catholicism and Republicanism, which made these two strands harmonious and all the more powerful for that fusion. The activists themselves became not merely men, but transcendent figures who would inevitably remind people of the religious figures they had known of since childhood, who had an emotional effect on them because of a mixture of those early memories and spiritual ideas.

When it came to the media representations of the hunger strikes, these tended to be local rather than national or international at first, given the use of censorship by the British. However, that local awareness gave the activists a local audience and sympathy that was perhaps more powerful because it was exclusive to a grassroots audience at that point. Later, when Bobby Sands died and the story was told further afield, even the most basic facts told a story of martyrdom and evoked a sense of tragedy, given Sands' age, his background, and the fact that he starved to death for his beliefs. Even the most hardened and distant audience would likely be concerned or ashamed that he suffered such a death. For even people who had no political sympathy, who were not of the same background and identity, would nevertheless recognise that story – that sense of tragedy and self-sacrifice that is ingrained in storytelling across cultures, and which explains, perhaps, why martyrdom is a theme used by political actors in so many different settings. The fusion of fame and suffering is one that seems to arrest audiences everywhere. Whatever the reason for this – be it voyeurism, deeply ingrained social ritual, confused admiration or sympathy – martyrdom is powerful as a political tactic and a narrative arc.

And yet the Conservative government at the time did not quite realise how powerful it could be. While Thatcher's rationale for ignoring the strikers was that any negotiations or change in status would "represent an acknowledgment of Irish Republican Army violence outside the prison" (Fierke, 107), this strategy backfired, partly because she underestimated the power of the hunger strikes from an emotional point of view. The self-sacrifice and deaths of the hunger strikers drew attention to their plight, drew attention to (and empathy towards) the victimhood of Catholics in Northern Ireland (especially given the symbolism inherent in the strikers' martyrdom), and ultimately encouraged support for the Provisional IRA in spite of their violence.

People were reminded of why these young men had joined the cause in the first place: a series of events in which Catholics were victimised, and peaceful protesters killed. In particular, the shooting of thirteen unarmed civilians during a demonstration in Derry in January 1972 (Bloody Sunday), by British paratroopers, had inspired young activists to abandon more peaceful means of dissent and join the Provisional IRA instead. As Bishop Edward Daly wrote in his memoirs *Mister, Are You a Priest?*: "Countless young people were motivated by the events of that day to become actively involved in armed struggle and, as a direct result, joined the Provisional IRA... Many former paramilitary members have gone on record stating that they first became actively involved in the wake of that Sunday. I am not at all sure about how I would have reacted, had I been a teenager and witnessed those same events" (Bowcott, 2010).

The hunger strikes reminded people of this sense of injustice and sympathy, and so the boys who died in Long Kesh were seen as victims rather than terrorists by many people. This perception was deepened by the symbolic nature of the deaths – not only the Catholic imagery of young men dying for their beliefs, but also more recent stories and communal memories of IRA resistance. Earlier in the 20th century, around the time of the 1916 Easter Rising, hunger strikes had been used as a political tactic, with over fifty strikes in the period between 1913 and 1923 (Sweeney, 1993; Fierke, 2014, 111).

The substance and history of the cause was exposed, the contemporary Provisional IRA was tied into a longer tradition of Irish Republicanism, and that helped its public image and suggested a more complex story than a simple 'good vs. evil' and the terrorism narrative of Thatcher's government and the British tabloids. The lines blurred, the characters, these 'terrorists', became first human, then saintly. And with this surge in public support, it became difficult for the British government to keep up its story that the Provisional IRA was a group of troublemakers with no real public support.

The British press, of course, used their expected language of condemnation and vitriol when covering the strikes and Sands' death, and underplayed the huge effect on public support. When Bobby Sands died of hunger, the *Daily Mail* called him out as guilty of "a moral fraud" and the *Daily Telegraph* called him "ruthless" and "corrupted". The *Express* dwelled on political failure: "Sands will find no victory in the grave... The shadow of Bobby Sands will pass...", while the *Sun* focused on the supposed victory of the British at his death: "Blackmail has failed... The society which has stood firm against violence in long blood-stained years will remain unshaken." At the news of Sands' funeral, the *Mirror* published an account that insisted Sands' funeral was "a pathetic end for a man who never played more than an average part in the deadly moves called by his IRA masters." The *Daily Mail* called it "a macabre propaganda circus" and "a gangster parody" (Greenslade, 2011).

Despite this coverage, Bobby Sands' death on 5th May 1981, at the age of 27, was not easily forgotten or dismissed – quite the opposite. Bobby Sands became a martyr to the cause – a secular saint, of sorts (Anderson, 2008). His story, and death, became known and mythologised not only in Northern Ireland but worldwide (Fierke, 2014, 107). Even the British press could not ignore him, especially since he was by this time an elected MP. While coverage of his death remained characteristically derisive, it nevertheless broke the censorship policy that had been in place before and hinted at the reality of public support for Sands and Irish Republicanism in general. Censorship, then, while an ideal for some governments in their dealing with dissent, even in the 1980s, before the Internet, was not always realistic in the face of particularly compelling personalities and their stories.

Sands, in this case, won a battle in the PR war between the British state and the Republican cause. Similarly, Nelson Mandela's transformation in the press from 'terrorist' villain to a symbol of peace and strength shows the way in which a government's strategy for dealing with the anti-establishment can be ineffective long-term, if community support (whether local or worldwide) is there. If the audience demands another narrative, or is compelled by one offered, then the story of censorship is less predictable than the state may hope. The state of course has learnt to work with that unpredictability; it has learnt to use publicity against its threats, when it cannot stifle it entirely. While bad publicity may be better than no publicity, it is still not ideal.

For dissenting groups, therefore, it is not just about getting publicity – it's about getting the right kind of publicity. It is necessary for the best narrative to dominate public discourse, and the cause therefore to win popular support, whether in the immediate locality, or further afield. Publicity, while important when it is the 'right' narrative, is not always 'oxygen for terrorists' when the state and wider establishment can control it. For many years the IRA, when it was mentioned, was portrayed in only negative and alienating terms. Bobby Sands' death marked a turning point in that he brought another layer to their story, and showed the Republican movement as sympathetic rather than merely villainous, but in general the British state and press were quite successful in cutting off publicity, and where that was impossible, in using it to make the Republican cause seem criminal and ridiculous. Indeed, despite Thatcher's statement about the "oxygen of publicity," the British establishment has more commonly used bad publicity as a sort of poisonous gas against dissent, rather than focusing entirely on censorship to cut off its 'oxygen'. Not only violent groups such as the Provisional IRA have been targets of this behaviour, but dissenting groups widely. Peaceful groups have also received a familiar combination of dismissal and demonisation to the more violent political actors.

Even high-profile dissent has been ineffective because of this combination of bad publicity and no publicity. As we saw with the Iraq protests of 2003, for instance, a million people marching did not change the government's mind, even though the event was highly publicised. The student protests of 2010, similarly, were ineffective in their aims, partly because media attention was generally focused on a small minority of rioters, who were demonised by the press. This is part of a wider trend, where anti-establishment groups are depicted in certain ways by the media, so that while their cause is given attention, it is not to their benefit. It is to the benefit of the establishment (politically), but also to media organisations who can make money from the political spectacle they air. There are clear commercial incentives for media organisations to cover the dramatic events of politics, whether terrorist attacks or protests, and we can see from recent history that media organisations have taken those opportunities. The media can be an ally as well as an enemy of dissenting groups. They can give publicity to a cause; but they can also make that cause look ridiculous, or that group's methods unreasonable. When a group receives media coverage of their actions, it can mean anything from political success to outright humiliation. Getting press can be far from useful; it is always a risk.

Media coverage of political violence, in particular, does not necessarily translate into 'success' for that cause. People may notice the group more, and be fascinated by them, but it doesn't mean they will sympathise with them at all. While media attention can raise morale for individuals in a group as well as recruit new people to it, while it can make members feel significant and relevant, that same coverage can outrage the public that sees it, and it can provide the provocation needed by a government to mobilise its military and other resources against that 'threat'. Importantly, media coverage means that the group is no longer secret, and with that new-found infamy comes scrutiny, aggression and criticism, all of which can be used to undermine and defeat them.

So although the media and dissent have evolved in parallel, the relationship is not always equal in its benefits. This largely depends on how media-savvy the dissenting group is. Infamy does not necessarily translate to political success, especially if the media organisation involved has some political interest itself – for example the British media during the IRA years; clearly they were swayed by British government interests (Whiting, 2012). However, as the IRA case showed, a group that understands this context, and can successfully manipulate the media to show itself in a sympathetic light, can benefit from media coverage as much as the media organisations themselves.

While the Irish revolutionary cause was Romantic in spirit in some ways, it was figures such as Bobby Sands who personified, quite intentionally, the sense of glory and tragedy that many people felt already about the Republican cause in Ireland, both at the time and historically. The hunger strikes made martyrs of Sands and his fellow prisoners, and a religious fervour surrounded them, for Sands' poetry and personality as much as any Catholic imagery. With instinct and intentional strategising, Sands created in himself the ultimate Romantic figure, doomed by an oppressive distant authority to a tragic and early death.

The hunger strikes were not simply a pose though; they articulated and expressed the way people (and these prisoners especially) felt about the Republican movement and its clash with the British and loyalists at that time. They were communicating not only their willingness to sacrifice themselves for a cause they believed in, but also the sense of victimhood they believed that the Republican cause could defend them against and ultimately put right. They were expressing a refusal to give up and give in to the British, even if it meant dying a long and painful death. They were showing that these men, and their cause, had a huge following, which refuted the British government's insistence, up until that time, that they did not. Perhaps most significantly, the strikes communicated that Sands and the other hunger strikers were not merely criminals, but political prisoners whom others could identify with and support. In expressing all of these things through the hunger strikes, the prisoners managed to change their public image, and that of Republicanism, through a compelling and emotionally charged message to the people as well as the British government. Theirs was a battle that merged Romanticism with *realpolitik* powerfully.

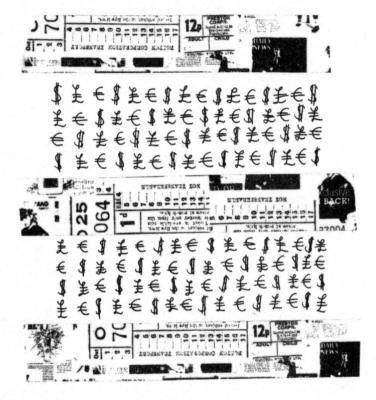

Chapter Three

The Business of Bad Publicity

It would be superficial to discuss media and dissent without examining their relations to government politics and business considerations, given that news agencies are influenced by their own business commitments as well as their allies in politics. Mainstream political actors clearly have an interest in working with the media, too, given the extent to which public opinion matters in a democracy (since the public vote in government). 'News management' is key in controlling who wins elections, and which issues get funding and support (Livingston, 1994). "A central function of some public administrative agencies is the publicizing of narratives about threats remote from daily experience, for these narratives create the rationale for intelligence organizations, national police agencies, and departments of defence" (Edelman, 1988).

If an administration wants to focus on high security and to fund war, for instance, then creating a scenario where the public also want high security or war is key. The publicity of dissent can work for government – perhaps more than it works for dissenting groups. Publicity relating to dissent can be oxygen for the establishment, often as it poisons dissent. Whether intentionally or not, Thatcher's statement was very misleading. The terrorism story can be great PR for the government, rather than mere advertisement for revolution.

Behind the Scenes

The relationship between dissent and the media, then, is one influenced by these other powers, as well as, possibly, an existing voyeurism of the public that dissent and media (and politics and business) all cater to. Governments often have an interest in influencing media organisations to cover dramatic political stories, particularly if they want to persuade the public to back policies and parties that push for high security measures and funding. In that vein, coverage of terrorist attacks is actually beneficial to some leaders, as highlighted by the paper 'Deliver Us From Evil: The Effects of Mortality Salience and Reminders of 9/11 on Support for President George W. Bush', which showed a rise in support for President Bush according to how often 'death' and specifically 9/11 were mentioned on television (Ogilvie et al, 2004). The threat of terrorism and the memory of it increased allegiance to the President and his government. The implication of this is that certain leaders and administrations have a major interest in the media's coverage of terrorism, given that it can sway public opinion in their favour, and increase the popularity of related security measures and other political decisions. If there is public expectation that 'more needs to be done' regarding terrorism, then not only the administration but the attached security forces (and involved businesses) benefit.

This may not be entirely beneficial to governments in the long term, however. Pressure on governments to react to specific attacks in a retributive, often unconsidered way, which may be disproportionate to the act itself, may be a problem for governments. Prime Minister John Major was asked about the effect of 'CNN Syndrome' on political decision-making in an interview and pointed out that: "I think it is bad for government. I think the idea that you automatically have to have a policy for everything before it happens and respond to things before you have had a chance to evaluate them isn't sensible" (Plate and Tuohy, 1993).

Whether or not a government benefits from dissent and its media coverage depends on the specific political intentions of that government. If a government wants to go to war and needs a way to persuade the public to back it, then a terrorist attack, widely publicised, is probably helpful as a means of persuading them. Furthermore, if a country is already at war, and needs to raise morale for its soldiers and the public, then demonising 'the enemy' via the media, and in response to particular catastrophes, can be helpful as it dehumanises them. This can work in the favour of the government in several ways: it makes violence seem sensible in an abstract sense (so that the population will not oppose military action, for instance), as well as on a more personal level. People in the military may have an easier time waging war on 'the enemy' if they have been convinced that their opponents are sub-human or not deserving of the same rights that they have or desire. Dehumanisation makes it possible for people to dispose of their own compassion and humanity; it is the perpetrator's humanity, in fact, that is undermined ultimately.

However, if a government does not have a way of benefiting from such dehumanisation, it can be pushed into emergency policies that are not good in the long term (or even short term) for the state. The manipulation of the content of the news, furthermore, undermines the integrity of journalism. What we are describing is not against 'freedom of expression', exactly, but it is a monopolisation of expression. The media exists not simply to further the objectives of government and business, and yet there are times when it can seem as if only government and business interests are really served, at the expense of true democracy and fair discussion. Whether one supports a dissenting group's cause or not, that the establishment should use the media against it (when it cannot censor it entirely) is some cause for concern for anyone attached to the most basic of democratic principles. The use of the media by any political actor, while inevitable perhaps, can blur the perception of the reality they propose to change, and hinder transparency and public debate. The public, should they wish to have any control, should exercise some critical viewing of the news, whether sympathetic to the government or dissenting groups, or any political actor. Otherwise, the public becomes merely an audience, taken in by the political spectacle, but effectively disengaged from the real issues behind it. The spectacle distracts from the important debate, from democracy itself. For dissenting groups, this means that they must be aware of the spectacle and, where necessary, learn to play in it for its own benefit. For individuals who wish only to see clearly the issues that engage them, they need to learn to see through the smoke and mirrors that all political actors are inevitably affected by.

How (and Why) Dissent is Re-framed

Propaganda is to a democracy what the bludgeon is to a totalitarian state. (CHOMSKY, 2002, 21)

As Chomsky has written, governments and businesses in liberal democracies cannot hold power over their own people through force in the way that they were able to a century ago, so 'public relations' was invented, so that those in government and business may control the people, since to control decision-making is to acquire power.

Even when dissenters capture the eye of the public,

through the media or otherwise, the government and its allies can usually transform this interest to repulsion and condemnation if they so wish. The public (when it becomes an audience) can be fickle, after all. The fictionalisation or dramatisation of terrorism (and counter-terrorism) means that information about the political issues at stake is more easily manipulated. Because such apparent conflict is seen as a story and a spectacle, no matter how serious the implications, the public opinion on those issues can be manipulated simply by framing the narrative a certain way – by sustaining the idea of all revolutionary action as 'evil' because it is 'terrorist', and all counter-terrorist action as 'good' because it is protecting national security.

Of course, there are competing interpretations of the story. As has been seen recently in the NSA scandal, the image of the counter-terrorists has been challenged, with the representation of counter-terrorism as unnecessarily intrusive becoming an important idea. The images that have emerged from Abu Ghraib, furthermore, showed another side of military intervention in the name of the War on Terror, as criminal and inhumane rather than heroic.

There is an on-going PR conflict when it comes to the establishment versus dissent narrative, which usually but not inevitably strengthens the state's position regarding revolutionary threats. This depends on revolutionary violence being termed 'terrorism', first of all, and on 'terrorism' more generally being portrayed as 'evil' in news media and fictional media. While 'terrorism' usually refers to violent dissent, the story of 'terrorism' and the fear of 'terrorism' taint the public image of all dissent in some way.

There is always a degree of risk when it comes to a PR stunt – whether it's a terrorist act or a celebrity endorsement –

because that stunt can be interpreted and received in so many ways, both flattering and detrimental to its cause (or client, if we're talking PR). A stunt may not have its intended effect, because how it is perceived, how it comes across, makes such a difference.

Usually, revolutionary action is framed in such a way as to strengthen the perception of the state, and to undermine the idea of revolution or dissent, as well as any possible reality of change through revolution. While the media may not be complicit with the establishment in an overt, explicit way, in effect it has been, for the most part, when we consider the way that revolutionary violence has been depicted in the media, and, conversely, the way in which state repression of dissent is glamorised in film and other fiction, but kept secret outside of that. Dissent and its repression is not, and never could be, represented with full accuracy, given the nature of the media and PR. So simply attracting attention to a cause and gaining public awareness is not enough; communicating the right or most persuasive message is vital. Politics and art have that much in common: an audience, and their hearts and minds to compel. Rhetoric matters as much as reality, style as much as substance.

New Media, Old Story

PR has changed and challenged dissent, then. Protesters are depicted as out-of-control, reckless youths, or unrealistic old hippies who never left the Sixties. Peaceful marches and occupations have been depicted as futile and more like festivals than political statements. Those who use violence and break the law, meanwhile, are demonised, perhaps called 'terrorists' or 'hacktivists', and threatened with draconian punishments and public wrath through the tabloids and the justice system. Meanwhile exhibitionists have used 'political' violence for attention – causing terrible loss of life but little if no political gains.

This refreshed emphasis on the public relations of dissent is partly because new media has changed the way we watch the news. Since censorship by the state (as in during the IRA years in the UK, or during the Cold War in the US also) is now particularly ineffective, the war of images and propaganda is more significant than ever. Giving a movement bad PR is the easiest way for a state or corporation to crush dissent.

In many ways, dissent has been hijacked by the media, and especially it's tendency to depict dissent as fashionable or exhibitionist rather than meaningful and political. When dissent is not presented as trivial, it is portrayed as demonic and evil. This is understandable when figures such as Osama bin Laden and Khalid Sheik Mohammed are linked to the deaths of thousands of people in terrifying attacks on civilians, or when groups such as ISIS post videos online of children beheading people, of innocent journalists being executed, and yet more civilians being killed because of their religion (if a cause is given). There are many atrocities that seem so horrendous that a word such as 'evil' seems the only one that can begin to describe the repulsion and dismay they inspire, and they happen daily. Some of this is committed by groups that are anti-establishment, or anti-Western, or anti-UK and -USA. Some of it is committed with a political justification spoken as it happens, or in amateur press videos afterwards. So we can, in many cases, link scenes of true horror to political groups and revolutionary individuals.

There are many occasions in which politics has a part in the provocation and justification of awful violence and it is unhelpful to ignore this fact when discussing dissent in a general sense. Sometimes political enemies carry out demonic acts against civilians and military targets alike. Sometimes, inevitably, certain movements do qualify as unethical and evil in their actions and disregard for human life. Sometimes those actions are in response to equally awful acts by our own states and others, and sometimes the reasons are more complicated.

To call out political violence as 'evil' is often a necessary and commendable thing to do. To criticise political enemies for their behaviour often makes sense. To abhor violence and to communicate that repulsion seems to me to be a natural reaction to learning of such events. But too often it does nothing to stop that violence or those perpetrators; rather, it fans the flames of animosity. It berates people who have not done anything terrible simply because they come from the same country or religion as those who have. This language, this naming of people as evil and alien and inhumane, does not stop violence; it is a form of dehumanisation itself and often divides people rather than helps build peace or reconciliation anywhere. It is one thing to renounce evil, but to stop there, to revel in denouncing evil, to obsess over how bad other people can be, seems to me unhelpful at best and provocative at worst. When it comes to the media, this naming and shaming can seem closer to a witch hunt than anything else, and in demonising political enemies, it runs the risk of fuelling further conflict.

A related problem is that in calling some anti-establishment figures evil, however justified that may be, as well as deepening divisions between people on various sides of a given conflict, we make it hard for people to understand that there are grey areas – that there are people neither good nor evil, and that there are complicated conflicts that cannot be easily simplified in such a way. Pointing to one event or person, calling them 'evil', and then using that to generalise and judge an entire people or cause, makes it very hard to negotiate or to understand that conflict on any other terms than the language of fairy tales.

There is also a tendency (already mentioned) for the media and state to generalise not only the people in one cause or group as dangerous, but to generalise all forms of dissent as dangerous simply because they are against the establishment. This is an overly simplistic approach to politics, clearly. It is damaging to those peaceful dissenting groups, but it is also damaging to the state, and to the public. It is a self-righteous and naïve position to take, to assume that any criticism against the establishment is bad or an existential threat, rather than a reasonable part of living in a democracy where debate about ways of doing things, ways of living, ruling and thinking should be open to discussion. Controlling what and who is acceptable, implying that every criticism is bad, makes that political debate tyrannical. It leaves no room for improvement, and makes for a paranoid and controlling state rather than a free one. While that probably appeals to some people in power, there are surely others who sleepwalk into positions of paranoia when it comes to dealing with anti-establishment thought within a democracy.

To take the most pragmatic viewpoint, this attitude leads to a waste of resources at the very least. Why waste so much money in training the police to deal with peaceful protesters as if they are lethal enemies of the state? Why spend so much money housing people in prisons when they could be contributing to society instead, for far less? Why assume that everybody who questions established thought and institutions is an enemy? It is all very well to treat actual threats to national security as such, but to extend this militarised defensiveness to deal with every stray end of debate is to risk falling into tyranny.

Even the use of the word 'terrorist' to describe certain perpetrators of political violence is problematic, and an example of the conflation of different forms of dissent. For a start, the word is rarely used to describe states – only political actors working separately to the state (even if they work for the state, indirectly, in proxy wars). So the word 'terrorist', although it refers to an attention-seeking tactic of war, is used only to describe anti-establishment warfare, rather than the various instances when similar behaviour is used by states in warfare, whether legally or not. Because the term 'terrorist' is used to mark out anti-state and sub-state groups, it becomes a way to say, "This cause is illegitimate," as well as shorthand for "these people are immoral, unreasonable and against us." It is a way of saying "we do not like them" (Jackson, 2005). It is a way to alienate and to 'other'.

While this may be all very well as a political tactic in itself, when the state is dealing with genuinely existential threats and wants to ensure mass repulsion of whatever cause they are dealing with, the word 'terrorist' is used to refer to other anti-establishment, dissenting groups. Even if they do not use terrorism as a tactic, or are not particularly threatening to the public or state, they are nevertheless lumped into the same broad category of public enemies and objects of state paranoia. Legislation such as the Terrorism Act (2006) means that individuals can be arrested and imprisoned for things like lending someone a publication that could "be useful in the commission or preparation of such acts and be understood, by some or all of those persons, as contained in the publication, or made available to them..." (Terrorism Act, 3b). This means that possession or distribution of a book that "glorifies the commission or preparation of such acts (whether in the past, in the future or generally)" (Terrorism Act, 4a) can be used to arrest and imprison someone, as that can be used to 'prove' intent. While proving intent is always complicated, proving it by pointing to one's book collection seems over the top.

The state uses surveillance not only on violent groups that threaten national security, but also on peaceful, democratic protest groups. Evidence has emerged that over the last several decades police officers were sent in to spy on various protest groups such as animal-rights groups, environmental groups, and left-wing groups, using the names of deceased children and (now infamously) engaging in intimate relationships with unknowing women for years. The Special Demonstration Squad spied on the family of Stephen Lawrence, as well as the families of other victims of alleged police brutality and racism (including Jean Charles de Menezes, the young Brazilian shot in the London Underground by police in 2005, and Cherry Groce, who was shot by police during the Brixton Riots of 1985). The unit itself was in operation from 1968 until 2008 (although this is no guarantee, of course, that such operations have ended at all). MI5, meanwhile, spied on left-wing academics such as Eric Hobsbawm and Christopher Hill, among many others, for decades (Milmo, 2014).

These people were often innocent, or at least not of grave threat to the country. And yet, the police and other government agencies considered it justified to spy on them. Sometimes this was for rather sinister reasons, such as worrying about information coming out about police brutality, or undermining left-wing sentiment in the country even if it represented no threat to democracy. CND activists and student protesters against education cuts, for example, seem largely unthreatening, and certainly pose no existential threat to the state or its principles (quite the opposite). At other times, the reasons were a little more complicated. While the aforementioned academics Hobsbawm and Hill may have been peaceful, the cause that they were associated with – the Soviet Union's Communism – was not. The state was perhaps justified in spying on a range of people it suspected of supporting their enemy, then.

Evidently when it comes down to justifying who is and who is not dangerous enough to watch and sabotage, the waters become rather murky. How can the state know who it should be against? How can it know whose data to collect and secrets to rifle through, when there is (nowadays more than ever) so much information, and such a range of possible threats?

While the state often has reason to be suspicious of certain dissenting groups, the problem is that it is not only genuinely dangerous threats (or associates of them) that are treated as such. Unfairly suspicious treatment towards peaceful groups and individuals is made possible by portraying various, or any, dissenting groups as related by some family resemblance, when often there is little connection and little threat.

This is a PR problem, insofar as it is the public image of the groups that is part of the issue, and helps justify excessive surveillance of peaceful and democratic groups alongside genuinely dangerous enemies of the state (such as Al Qaeda or ISIS, these days). When groups are depicted as against the state, against the country, or even just associated with those who are, then the public does not leap to their defence if they are undermined by those in authority and treated undemocratically. Public relations is not generally the reason why some people and groups are targeted, but when they are targeted, bad PR can make the difference between the public

caring about the infringement of civil liberties and democratic rights, and not caring at all. While there are times when
the state's action against dissenting groups is justified (for
example, when there really is an existential threat to the state
and people in it), there are also many instances when people
are treated unfairly, and rhetoric that places them all in the
same category of threat means that the public does not know
the difference or think to question that action. Too often, the
phrase "for the sake of national security" is used to denounce
groups that pose no such threat at all.

There has been some talk lately of how 'new media' has
changed dissent. As Neville Bolt has written in *The Violent
Image* (2012), dissenting groups (he focuses broadly on insur-
gents) have greater means to control their public image,
because the Internet makes censorship less effective and
less of a realistic strategy for dealing with 'insurgent propaganda', or letting one side of the story dominate. Indeed,
Al Qaeda benefited from its use of social media in the sense
that it enabled communications and recruitment via Internet
forums and the distribution of radical material, such as its
magazine, *Inspire*. But as Gilbert Ramsay has explained (2015)
this use of the Internet does not always, or even often, lead
to actual political violence. Extremism and what is known
as 'terrorism' are distinct, and the former does not always
lead to the latter. So although the Internet is, as it is for most
industries and groups, a resource, it is not quite as terrifying or game-changing as is sometimes implied. This is worth
remembering when, for instance, people talk of the need to
increase surveillance and prison sentences and impose other
controls, with that supposed connection as justification.

The Internet is threatening to the establishment in other
ways, though. The Abu Ghraib scandal showed how a few

leaked pictures could change the image of a superpower, very much against its wishes and its own rules. So the new media, in that respect, has changed the original 'oxygen for terrorists' strategy: if publicity is oxygen then the state cannot so easily cut it off. What is interesting though is that it is not necessarily the propaganda of terrorist groups (or protest groups) that the state need worry about; rather it is exposure of the state's own misadventures and illegal activity that is most damaging and thus threatening. Understandably, though, the state does not use this as its justification for attempts to control the new media; it uses the familiar excuse that demonic 'terrorists' lurk in the Dark Net; they must be stopped, they must be cut off...

So has 'new media' really changed the dynamic? Or is it merely the next chapter in a rather consistent story, where, censorship or no censorship, dissent is framed as 'bad', no matter its specific characteristics or tactics, and the establishment is framed as 'good', no matter the secrets it hides? Does it matter that censorship is less realistic, if all publicity is bad publicity (for dissent), and if the story remains the same?

The old story, the tale of good versus evil in a spectacular political theatre, persists. It resonates partly because the audience – the public – likes the simplicity and sensationalism of this story. They like to be part of the winning side, and for complicated issues to be conveniently simplified as 'good' against 'bad'. They like to be good. They like to be titillated by bad.

New media has not changed this. The same narratives run on; they have merely been adapted to a new medium, much like an old classic being re-released as digitally re-mastered and sold over again. The 'old media', meanwhile, has not really gone anywhere. People still read the tabloids in print, as well as online, and the stories are the same. Often, the social media presence of dissenting groups can be their undo-ing, anyway. Twitter accounts have been used as evidence for 'inciting violence' and terror; Facebook profiles give motives to police; and iPhone signals make public enemies easily trackable. While social media and the Internet more generally can be an asset to dissenting groups, they can be even more useful to those government or corporate agents who wish to contain them. The mainstream media, whether 'new' or 'old', persists with its power, then. Bad publicity is a business and an art.

With all of this in mind, dissenting groups face myriad problems, or opportunities, when it comes to communicating their messages to the public. Perhaps the main issue is rec-ognising how easy it is for one's actions to become merely a strange form of entertainment, rather than having any polit-ical effect. A group can slip into this situation whether it is violent or peaceful, whether it embraces old or new media, and whether it really poses a danger to the government or not. No matter how convincing a group's ideas may be, if it does fall into this trap, and if it is represented negatively, then the public will never be swept up in its vision. It is neces-sary to understand the theatrical nature of politics, and how to approach it so that it is of benefit rather than detriment to one's cause.

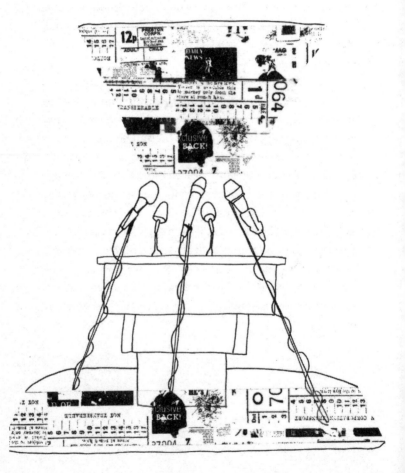

Chapter Four
The Political Spectacle

Since the advent of photography, war, for the home front, has been more than romantic dreams and glorious slogans. Battle has become something in which everyone participates – if only in absentia. The camera has brought the exotic and the dangerous near; it satisfies a lust for seeing the action, with the bonus that the viewer at home is never in any danger. Like the voyeurs of the past century who drove their carriages out to a hillside to watch the battle below, the armchair audience gazes at, but does not participate in, war… For civilians combat is a vicarious experience composed of certain moments observed second hand in the pages of the press. (MOELLER, 1989, 3)

These days political theatre is alive and well in the new as well as the old media. ISIS produces politically violent snuff movies; tabloid and 'broadsheet' papers (online and in print) such as the *Daily Mail* and the *Guardian* describe the downfall of political enemies with caricature-ish venom and the language of Hollywood action films. The events they depict, moreover, appeal to such reports: public violence such as hangings (Saddam Hussein), shoot-outs and assassinations (the Boston Bombers, Osama bin Laden) are spectacular as action films, the theatrical nature of which is amplified for a global audience with the media's take on the 'news'.

There is good reason for this tendency, apart from the ideological loyalties of particular newspapers and broadcasters, and the complimentary PR ideas of Western governments and dissenters alike. These stories sell because they are, it would seem (given the many people who watch), entertaining. And so they make money. There is a commercial reason to give attention to dissent, quite removed from the political causes that these groups may be trying to communicate, and it is connected to the audience's voyeurism rather than their interest in the political issues and injustices of the day.

Violence as an Art / Art as Violence

Violence as communication is nothing new, not only in political communication such as war and political activism, but in art, comedy, and areas that combine them all. The Marquis de Sade wrote much about the connections between sadomasochism and art: the art of inflicting pain, the design of violence. Thomas De Quincey, also, wrote about 'the art of murder' in *On Murder Considered as One of the Fine Arts* (1827), reflecting on whether there is really a difference between crime and art. Oscar Wilde was also well versed in such ideas of decadence, the meeting place between violence and art. These are all intriguing notions, and although they have often been taken as provocative essays intended to amuse and titillate, the ideas they discuss are relevant to the issue of violence as communication, and the readiness of people to engage with such a 'dialogue'.

Indeed, it would seem that people find some pleasure in the suffering of others – whether that's because it means that their own misfortunes seem lesser in comparison, or because of a more sadistic impulse, or simply because there is some entertainment value in any drama, no matter if or how someone gets hurt. Shock value and the draw of the spectacle seem to engage people across societies and times – in art as in life – and therefore in media, too: in that fusion of the two.

If people enjoy depictions of violence in art – in films, plays, novels, and television – then where does this 'artificial' violence meet real violence? Do people know the difference, if it is not happening to them, if they are not personally subjected to violence? Sontag makes the point that whether the violence is seen through a photograph or in real life, the important point is that the viewer is watching, rather than a perpetrator or a victim. The viewer cannot truly empathise with either, as has been suspected (or hoped); he or she cannot know what it feels like to be the victim of violence, to experience it first-hand. So there is a misplaced sense of reaction to violent spectacles, perhaps, when people are shocked or emotionally affected in some way, but assume that they are being empathetic. Sontag implies that this supposition of 'empathy' is not true empathy, or at least, it can only go so far, and possibly conceals an emotional reaction that is in fact some sort of curiosity or voyeurism. As Sontag puts it: "Images have been reproached for being a way of watching suffering at a distance, as if there were some other way of watching. But watching up close – without the mediation of an image – is still just watching" (Sontag, 2003, 105).

If this is so, then perhaps there is something about violence that draws emotional reaction from viewers, and that has little to do with empathy, which can better be described as sensationalism. While the link between media, art and sensationalism, or the sensational, is a complicated one, we can at least say that sensationalism is a derivation of (or deviation from) art. As propaganda is known to employ similar techniques to art in order to engage attention and manipulate thoughts, so does sensationalism. Terrorism, we could say, is a particularly sensationalist form of propaganda – its violence is, and so are depictions of that violence. And there is an art to it, even if we cannot describe violence as an art form exactly. Violence, especially if it happens to engage an audience, is creative, self-conscious, and sensationalistic. It is emotionally manipulative, coercive, and, at times, is entertaining to people on account of drawing these reactions.

Apart from being sensational, violent images can also be beautiful, or sublime, in a more straightforward way. If a violent scene is captured with symmetry and attention to detail, with good composition and expressive faces, then perhaps it is inevitable that people will find it compelling – perhaps all the more so for originating in something horrific and otherwise repellent:

> The landscape of devastation is still a landscape. There is beauty in ruins. To acknowledge the beauty of photographs of the World Trade Center ruins in the months following the attack seemed frivolous, sacrilegious. The most people dared say was that the photographs were 'surreal', a hectic euphemism behind which the disgraced notion of beauty cowered. But they were beautiful, many of them... The site itself, the mass graveyard that had received the name, 'Ground Zero', was of course anything but beautiful. Photographs tend to transform, whatever their subject; and as an image something may be beautiful — or terrifying, or unbearable, or quite bearable — as it is not in real life. (Sontag, 2003, 68)

It is not surprising, then, that people will be impressed or dazzled by spectacular violence, even if they are also appalled by it. The problem, of course, is that violence usually has victims, and when people treat it as entertainment, however accidentally, they deny its seriousness. In making a spectacle of suffering, violence is made to appear less 'real', and the reality of suffering is therefore denied through its objectification.

That voyeurism, of course, affects the political issues of the day. It is partly responsible for the mass consumption of sensationalist tabloids that run these stories, and sustains a movie industry that exploits the same popular narratives and simple plots. That movie industry – those films – in turn influence how the public sees political actors, and especially those who rebel against the establishment. Life is swayed by art (the term used broadly here); the public learns politics at least in part from Hollywood action movies and dramatic tabloids.

In turn, Hollywood films use political drama, and dissent especially, as the subjects of films, for entertainment value as well as, perhaps, political allegiance. Whether to affect catharsis or not, these mainstream films tend to cast dissenters, generally, in villain roles, and the establishment's security agents in hero roles. James Bond, for example, though fond of heavy drinking, womanising, and gratuitous and exhibitionist violence, is held up as a hero, while dissenters are for the most part, no matter their cause, regarded as irrational and immoral (for example the depiction of IRA members in *Patriot Games*, or Baader Meinhof in *The Baader Meinhof Complex*). While of course some political violence may be irrational or immoral, the stereotypical treatment of all dissent as possessing these qualities is a misrepresentation of many groups in question, and misses the interesting subtleties of the politics and people involved (even if some of the films are entertaining and perhaps aesthetically valuable). It is unusual for dissenting groups, whether violent and illegal, or peaceful and legal, to benefit from their Hollywood adaptations, however. Rather, it is a central problem for dissenters and revolutionary or subversive groups that they are usually typecast in the villain roles, and the establishment are handed out roles as the 'good guy'.

The Bad Guys

We are surrounded by baddies – there are probably more 'terrorists' in films than in reality. From the various enemies of James Bond, to Abu Nazir (and the 'enemy within', Brody) in *Homeland*, to every hitman, psychopath and mindless rebel in a Western spy thriller, these baddies are often revolutionaries, or dissenters of some persuasion, given a devilish makeover. And people enjoy this performance. Often the performance extends to real life, as well, where individual dissenters are treated as if they are real-life pantomime villains. Whether guilty of a serious crime or not, political villains are treated with similar levels of disdain – be it Saddam Hussein or bin Laden, Jimmy Saville or Margaret Thatcher, Heather McCartney Mills or Abu Hamza, Alex Salmond or 'Jihadi John' – once a villain, always a similar role.

With this typecasting there comes a special kind of dehumanisation – one that sees people as merely characters in a play, and thus not 'human' in the usual sense. A demon is not a person, just as a celebrity, or a saint, has become transcendent too. Once a person is cast in a role by society, he or she is not thought of as strictly human, but above or below human. For dissenters, violent or not, they are usually thought of as subhuman. For celebrities, there are ups and downs of course, but there is a little more scope to be glamorously untouchable than damned forever by the press.

This dehumanisation of course often reaps political benefits (in the case of celebrities and dissenters alike, for the TV producers and executives more than the lowly actors). Even revolutionary violence can be framed in such a way as to strengthen the image of the establishment. Both revolutionary and state propaganda works by dramatising violence so that damage is dehumanised, dramatic and symbolic, aiming to influence the political narrative, by defining (or redefining) what is 'good' and 'evil' according to their own political ideas. Dehumanisation is key to propaganda, whichever side is controlling its narrative arc, because it simplifies the complexities of human conflict to basic 'good' versus 'evil' ideas; a simple pantomime logic that is easily understood and consumed by the public.

The Good Guys

The figure of the counter-terrorist is as significant and prevalent in modern culture and politics as the 'terrorist', the rebel or the dissenter, and of course as significant in the dynamics of political, revolutionary violence itself. From James Bond to Carrie Matheson in *Homeland*, to *Spooks* and *Jack Ryan*, covert agents are not hidden from popular culture. Rather, they are as much a part of the dissent narrative as the terrorist. They are the 'good' to the revolutionary's 'evil', even when the protagonists' morals are questionable. In *Homeland* the various CIA agents featured are shown battling moral dilemmas, more often than not picking the apparently immoral choice, depicted as a kind of self-sacrifice that is necessary to protect national security. The ambiguous moral character of these 'counter-terrorists' is part of their attraction, however, when politics is entertainment, and character flaws add to the suspense. This suspension of disbelief and simple psychological understanding are fine when it comes to watching a film in the evenings. It is when these perceptions become the way that the public understands real political issues that the problems start. 'The Good Guys' and 'The Bad Guys' are not real; they are an over-simplification of political issues and individuals, and a distraction from them.

How do depictions of counter-terrorists – whether in fiction or in the news media – relate to the reality of counter-terrorism, then? The most obvious point is that most of it is unknown, because most of it is concealed. Of what has been exposed or revealed, we know that torture has been used by counter-terrorists, as well as interrogation techniques that border on torture. We know that surveillance is a crucial part of counter-terrorism – phone-tapping, secret cameras, hacking into email and Internet use. Undercover operations are another part of counter-terrorist work, though rather than taking a few hours or weeks, as they seem to when fictionalised, these operations can go on for years.

For the most part, the work is secret, which is why the construction of counter-terrorism as including figures such as James Bond is problematic. Even if James Bond is supposed to be secret (within the story), we only know of counter-terrorism as a drama, so the 'secretive' nature of the work is not taken entirely seriously. That spies exist seems to be part of a suspension of disbelief. Counter-terrorism cannot be understood as secretive and covert, really, because nearly every representation of it is fictional, or imbued with fictional connotations, and furthermore it is dramatised.

This has the effect of undermining the pervasive nature of counter-terrorism, the freedoms given to the security services and military personnel. Films such as the *James Bond* franchise affect a kind of denial in the public, or a distraction at least, from the reality of counter-terrorism as pervasive, hidden, intrusive and often mundane rather than endlessly dramatic, heroic and glamorous. That counter-terrorism is usually put on a pedestal often puts it beyond proper discussion, similarly to revolutionary action. By being a drama above all, both terrorism and counter-terrorism do not seem entirely real to the general population, and so the issues they represent are not taken as seriously. Dissent is disregarded, often, because it is not thought about or engaged with so much as watched as part of a wider political theatre, where rebellion does not usually have a happy ending.

Entertainment as Politics: An Old Story

Of course some groups can and do exploit this state of affairs, and use the media – new and old – to make political statements. Of recent years, ISIS have emerged, with their snuff movies and disturbing pastiches of Hollywood horror films, as experts in the field. They use a sadistic form of entertainment to attract new recruits and intimidate their enemies. Their various videos of beheadings, burnings and executions are grisly, and alienate many people, but also attract the attention and sometimes admiration of their target audiences, and terrorise the rest. Their 'PR strategy' is to disarm as well as to entertain, depending on who is watching. More than other groups, they have used new media effectively to communicate their 'message', or to terrorise their enemies, and more than other groups, they have won the attention of old media also. They show that whether old or new, the story of terrorism works as it always has done.

Would ISIS have been so infamous without the Internet, though? While they would probably not have chosen these specific methods, such as political snuff films, they would nevertheless have been a force to be reckoned with. ISIS are more than their PR strategy after all. But their ability to use YouTube and create content that attracts attention, however horrifically, complements that existing power. ISIS have adapted well to an age where PR matters, and are up-to-date with developments in the media, but that does not fully explain their power and influence. Social media presence is not enough; it requires existing 'real' power, usually through ties to an established political actor, behind the scenes.

Conversely, several recent dissenting groups have attempted to use new media to their benefit, and have failed to do so effectively. While social media was used to rouse support for anti-austerity protests, including various Occupy demos and sit-ins, the information was freely available and used to undermine those movements by police, and indirectly by the press. This was not because their PR was especially bad, but because it was easily sabotaged and ignored by a mainstream media without any interest in or loyalty to their cause. More importantly, the cause did not have enough support. (This will be discussed further in chapter four.) Public Relations is not all there is to politics; a group needs substantial political support, whether grassroots, connections to an established power, or a mixture of both, as well as good PR, to be successful.

The existence of new media does not change the essential dynamic of dissenting groups, their image in the public eye, or the power of the establishment, whether in support of them or against them. And while public relations must be understood as one tactic among several, it is nevertheless important to find out the circumstances in which it works best. Getting attention for a cause, as this book has already shown, is not a simply matter of 'all publicity is good publicity'; it is more complicated than that. By examining the different approaches various groups have taken, we can learn what works and what doesn't, and uncover the wider issues that affect a group's image and success. We need to take a closer look at the specific ways dissenting groups approach PR and the media, and learn from them, whether we are sympathetic to their politics or not. Groups and causes this book will focus on therefore include quite a broad range: from Occupy and various anti-austerity groups in the UK to the Tea Party Movement, from Al Qaeda (and affiliated individuals and groups) to ISIS, Anonymous, WikiLeaks and the Stop the War Coalition.

In writing this book, I want to find out what dissenting groups need to do (and in some cases have done) to be taken seriously, and I'm discussing a wide range of groups to assist in this. To answer the central question, I will also need to discuss the following key issues that affect how dissenting groups relate to the media, defining the choices they make regarding publicity, tactics and long-term success: should they be violent or non-violent? Legal or illegal? Internet-focused or a physical presence? Public or clandestine? Referencing four main groups of dissent (grouped together according to their PR strategies), I hope to find out what the best course of action is for a dissenting group: what to do, and what not to do. While all publicity might be good publicity for those chasing fame, it is not true of groups who want to affect political change. While I certainly do not support or sympathise with all the groups I will go on to discuss, I am equally interested in how they have approached PR and how they relate to the public, and want to know how these findings can be applied to groups I do sympathise with – those democratic and peaceful groups that get undermined by bad PR and a gradual infringement of freedom of press and other civil liberties.

Chapter Five

The Stylish Kids in the Riot

During the 2010 anti-austerity protests and student protests (against cuts to education and rises in tuition fees), the media tended to focus on the small minority of protesters who engaged with violence, rather than the thousands of peaceful protesters. Publishing images of a seemingly terrified Charles and Camilla, broken glass, fires being set and Molotov cocktails being thrown, the news showed chaotic scenes of drama and violence, above scenes of peaceful marches and sit-ins. In so doing, the protests were misrepresented, and draconian punishments were presented as justified. Dissent was not only trivialised, in the representation of out-of-control students, but also condemned, and the movement was therefore damaged, being seen by many as illegitimate on account of this public image.

The Occupy movements in the US as well as the UK were given similar treatment by the press (as detailed further in the next chapter). Depicted as a sprawling mess of students, unemployed people and hippies, in a throwback to the 1960s, the group was dismissed and ridiculed by the press when it was not entirely ignored. The general impression seemed to be that the Occupy movement was chasing an impossible dream, that its days were numbered, and that it was a nuisance to those whose stroll to work was interrupted (in the case of Occupy Wall Street). That a lot of the occupations took place in universities (for example UCL, Cambridge, Oxford, LSE, Leeds and many others) only compounded an image of the protests as trivial and naïve. This was the idea communicated to the public – not the politics behind the action, and not the demands. Films of students sitting in occupied university buildings with sleeping bags and rucksacks give an impression of a festival, especially when the political discussions and organisation cannot be heard alongside. Photographs of protestors being detained and 'caught' meanwhile – even when no laws had been broken – give an image of lawlessness and chaos regardless.

Arguably these press portrayals (as well as dismissal in the form of withholding publicity) led to the police repression of these peaceful protests being seen as justified and sensible. When Occupy Wall Street was dismantled, and Zucotti Park /Liberty Plaza was raided by police, however, those involved remained positive:

> Following the example of police in other cities, the NYPD entered the camp under cover of night and evicted all the residents, confiscating tents, sleeping bags, and books, and pepper-spraying and arresting protesters. In response to these attacks occupiers posted a message online. "You can't evict an idea whose time has come," it began. Rebecca Solnit put it more poetically: "You can pull up the flowers, but you can't stop the spring." (Taylor, Gessen, et al (eds.), 2011, vii)

This is a hopeful metaphor, and inspiring resilience, but it is of course possible to quash dissent in a way one can't change the seasons. Success, after all, is not inevitable. While protest, especially that which is recorded well, as the Occupy movement has been, may never be forgotten, and stands at the very least as a record of political discontent and moral principle, it is all too possible for such movements to be politically ineffective in the long run on account of bad press, public disapproval and subsequent or connected repression.

While protests and occupations were being broken up, meanwhile, advertising and pop culture co-opted the idea of dissent – with the controversial Levi's advert, for example, which saw people wearing their brand of jeans in a riot, the M.I.A. pop video depicting another violent riot (with red-heads rising up), not to mention the infamous Stephen Meisel shoot in *Vogue Italia*, showing a girl in handcuffs and implications of torture, in his feature 'State of Emergency'. Dissent was presented as fashionable and dangerous, but not politically effective.

The protests were ultimately unsuccessful for various reasons, the most significant being that the protesters, whether peaceful or not, were portrayed negatively. In this context of advertising campaigns and pop videos that sensationalised the idea of protest, this had the ultimate effect of making the politics seem trivial to the spectacle. Individual protesters were focused on, and usually demonised, at the expense of the many other protesters who were ignored despite their presence (in their tens of thousands). There were only negative, worrying stories; there were no heart-warming counter-narratives, no inspirational figures, and certainly no serious discussion of politics (other than 'how to contain dissent', or 'how to punish the wild students'). The kids were out of control; the protests were depicted, at their best, as a school trip gone wrong, or a student rave spilled out into the day-lit hours.

More anxiety-inducing stories gave an impression of a nightmarish rebellion by ne'er-do-wells, thankfully quashed by the ever-heroic police. The stories of police brutality – for instance Alfie Meadows, who had to receive emergency brain surgery after being battered by a police officer – received minimal coverage. A protester at the same march, however, received far more attention, for some reckless behaviour that led to no physical harm – no life-threatening injuries or abuse of police power. And yet Charlie Gilmour became something of a poster boy of the protests for some antics involving a Cenotaph. The subsequent public hysteria went some way to ensuring months in jail and a protracted media obsession with a young man whose only criminal conviction was 'violent disorder', or rather, some badly timed vandalism (he smashed a window in Topshop).

The police officer who injured Alfie Meadows never became known or vilified in the press; there was no massive outcry at the victim's experience, no pursuit of the perpetrator. But Charlie became a hate figure overnight – his photographs in every national newspaper, his friends hounded by journalists vying for a scoop, his family sent hate mail. His demonisation in the press was worrying enough; that the entire movement was dismissed on account of that demonisation even more so. Charlie was disrespectful to a monument, but it was not damaged, and no lives were lost. And yet he was hounded and vilified in much the same way that a terrorist would be in the press; he was sent to prison for it.

Charlie may not have made the best PR move that day, but the press' reaction to his actions exposed a ridiculous bias against protest, and specifically its tendency to conflate peaceful protest with 'terrorism'. It also betrayed a dangerous hypocrisy, whereby police brutality was ignored, but entire front pages were dedicated to the misadventures of a rogue protester. If any good should come from that day it is to learn something about the way the media works, to understand that protest can be a limited tool for dissenting groups, when the mainstream media is skewed against them using that democratic right. The papers, as the next chapter will show, seem generally to be more interested in playing pantomime and destroying whoever happens to be cast as the villain, than in representing democratic protest fairly. Perhaps that should be an obvious point, but it is one often missed by peaceful dissenting groups especially. Although it varies from case to case, it may be that sometimes the best PR is no PR.

So what of the protesters who are shot down for being too hip? For being too idealistic and unprofessional? What of the stylish kids at the riot and the riotous kids at the protest – what are we to do with them? Should we disown them and distance ourselves? Should we be brutal in our insistence that we strategise in reaction to the state's hold on PR? Each movement will make its own decisions, but I would think that generally we should hold back on being too prescriptive and self-censoring. This book has outlined what tends to work, but it has not said what to do when things nevertheless don't work, when we get PR wrong. It shouldn't matter as much as it does, but it does. So again, what of those romantics, ruffians and trouble-makers? Do we stand by them, or march on without them? I may betray my own Romantic sentiments, but I would have some solidarity in those occasions, some camaraderie. I would think that we would be losing something important simply to focus only on strategy and not on one another. Rather than criticise and scapegoat those who are demonised by the press, perhaps it makes more sense to organise protest and dissent more generally in such a way that the press cannot so easily bring down individuals and a movement with them.

This takes foresight and analysis as much as emotional commitment and camaraderie – each is as necessary as the other. It makes no sense either to abandon true solidarity for the sake of perfecting (or trying to perfect) a public image, just as it is better to avoid the excesses of a movement's Romantic spirit at the expense of communicating ideas to the public with any clarity or persuasion.

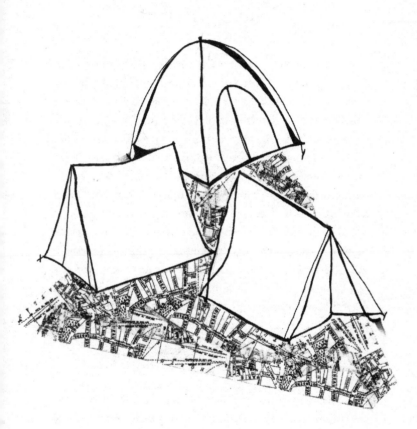

Chapter Six
Populist Dissent

Populist movements such as the Tea Party movement, Occupy, Stop the War, and others rely on popular, community support, and mainstream media coverage of their protests and political arguments. Though very different politically, Occupy and the Tea Party movement have relied on similar PR techniques, to varying success. They have both used public protest, they have both utilised social media, and they have both relied on grassroots support. They have also both faced similar animosity from the government, given that both were opposed to the government, albeit in quite different ways. As time went on, Occupy suffered from negative and alienating portrayals in the press. While the Tea Party had less of a problem with this, the interest in the movement from big business ultimately undermined its credibility and it was arguably absorbed into the Republican Party – the very people it was (mostly) against.

Occupy

As mentioned in the previous chapter, Occupy fell into the trap (as did Stop the War, Uncut, among many other groups) of being mocked as hipsters and dirty hippies, therein causing disruption and mess. As Jacob Greene for *Solidarity US* noted: "Many reports were redolent with discussions of the protesters' waste, including everything from their trash and camping debris to their actual urine and faeces" (Greene, 2011). Greene points to an interview on CNN with Peter Greene, where he characterises the Occupy movement thus: "The entire tone of the demonstrations at Zucotti Park... living in their own faeces and urine" (King, CNN, 17/11/11). He also discusses a Fox News report in which the TV host Greg Gutfeld describes the protesters themselves as waste: "[The Los Angeles Sanitation Department hauled away] thirty tonnes of waste, and that's not including the protesters!"

Various media reports of violence came to represent the movement in the mainstream, as opposed to its extensive reach, support and careful organisation. There was a tendency to fixate on rare instances of violence that happened during a protest, even if it was not connected to it. In November 2011, for instance, near an Occupy camp in Philadelphia, a 50 year-old man raped a 23 year-old woman. The *Blaze* reported that: "Sexual assaults and other violent incidents have been reported at a number of Occupy Wall Street camps around the country, though Philadelphia's has been fairly peaceful, according to WPVI. The movement has been criticized for its responses to sexual assaults, particularly at Occupy Baltimore where it distributed pamphlets discouraging victims from coming forward to the police, instructing them instead to report incidents to the 'Security Team'" (Morgenstern, 2011). Although Occupy Baltimore refuted claims that their pamphlets discouraged victims from reporting violence (Lewis, 19/10/2011), the *Blaze* article did not offer readers that comeback, or in fact Occupy statements or explanations regarding many alleged crimes and problems. Even when, in the case of the *Baltimore Sun* for example, a fuller story was offered (Hermann, 2011), the press nevertheless tended to report only on problems and negative developments within Occupy, rather than anything positive. The portrayal of Occupy demos and the wider movement was overwhelmingly negative, with a tendency, also, for papers and magazines to connect one instance of violence to every other known instance of alleged violence at any Occupy protest, anywhere.

A picture built up, therefore, of a reckless and dangerous movement in which young women were vulnerable to abuse, and people were unprotected by the movement itself as they were living lawlessly. While it was true that some occupations were attempting to self-govern and even experiment with alternative systems of reporting crimes or dealing with disputes, in the spirit of a new, more direct and communal form of democracy, this was picked up by the press and shown to be reckless, dangerous and harmful, rather than responsibly innovative.

Another interesting tendency in the press was to connect the Occupy movement with the Arab Spring, and even the threat of 'terrorism'. As Heather Horn wrote in the *Atlantic*: "There's a strong tendency in certain national presses to see Occupy as part of a global protest trend. Much of the language of the Occupy Wall Street protests, of course, has encouraged this, and protesters might be pleased to note the movement's invocation of the Arab Spring" (Horn, 2011). While protesters might have liked the comparison, in the context of a country worried about threats from the Middle East, due to the media obsession with the threat of 'terrorism', being associated with 'political dissent in the Middle East' probably wasn't conducive to mainstream, public support. The comparison worried people, and enabled a connection between Occupy's mainly peaceful protests, and worldwide riots in the name of ideas a lot of people didn't understand and didn't consider relevant to their own lives.

In this way, then, a movement concerned with local, direct action, became linked to a global problem and a threat of national insecurity. The notion that Occupy was an 'anti-American' movement was particularly unhelpful for the group (King, 2011). As Peter Lehr has argued, groups that are seen to be incorrigible threats, such as groups whose ideas will challenge the establishment, are treated with more repression (from the state as well as established, mainstream media) than groups whose violence does not threaten the *status quo*. As Lehr has shown, right-wing groups generally do not receive the same kind of repression as left-wing groups, because while they are a serious threat to individuals, or even whole sections of society, they don't threaten the police or the government. Lehr also points out that, as a consequence of seeming more threatening, left-wing groups are 'othered' more than right-wing groups, with the latter still being included as 'us' (Lehr, 2013, 188).

So while Occupy was a populist movement, the support it had was undermined by the media portraying it as 'other', and as threatening to the American identity (in the case of the US Occupy groups). A populist group needs to be seen to represent much more than a hippy minority. Although Occupy obviously tried to appeal to (nearly) everyone with its slogan "We are the 99%", even this was undermined by the media focusing on whatever qualities supposedly made them 'other': dirtiness, youth, and a link to ideas popular with people in other countries – ironically, in the case of the Arab Spring, a form of democracy. Perhaps part of the reason for the public's tendency to accept this narrative was that many people, while part of the 99% that Occupy tried to bring together, did not want to be associated with that multitude, and were more loyal to the 1% they aspired to be rather than the 'masses' along with everyone else. In a country tradition-ally bewitched by tales of the American Dream, it could be that the 99% (or a strong majority, anyway) prefer to identify themselves as followers of that dream rather than subjects of a poorer reality.

The Tea Party Movement

The Tea Party movement emerged around about the same time as Occupy, and had similar grievances, to a point. Both were discontent and distrustful of an apparent 'political elite' and corruption in banking and big business. The ideas they followed (in both Occupy and the Tea Party) have a long tradition in the US – a country founded on revolution, after all, and (on both sides of the political spectrum) a distrust of the idea of a corrupt, out-of-touch government.

> Our country is in the midst of a massive, unprecedented, underreported, underappreciated, new populist revolt that has emerged overwhelmingly from the right, manifesting itself as Tea Party movement... as well as a smaller, and probably less significant reaction on the left. The means of expression for these two strands varies, as does the ideology that underlies the sentiments they cacophonously voice. Yet, together they comprise the new populist revolt. (Rasmussen and Schoen, 2010, 19)

But while Occupy envisioned a new, more 'in touch' and democratic form of government as the solution, the Tea Party movement disagreed on this point and sought to limit government, to undermine its power. Interestingly, in this case, the right-wing Tea Party movement was a threat to government in its ideology, and so there was a greater degree of government repression than perhaps most right-wing groups would have received, in line with Lehr's observations about the usually 'corrigible' rather than 'incorrigible' threat from the right. However, the US government (and the media) nevertheless dealt with the Tea Party and Occupy in quite different ways. While Occupy was often ignored or dismissed as a group of frivolous, naïve (and dirty) hippies, the Tea Party was given more approval in press (though Tea Party members have also complained of being misrepresented by the mainstream media).

This was helped by a perhaps more explicit effort to avoid violence and 'mess' by the Tea Party organisers, in part because they saw how an association with these negative traits (whether true or not) had affected the public image of the Occupy movement. As Paul Ibbetson, the Master of Ceremonies (and PR man) of the Kansas Tea Party, explained:

> I think from the get go, the media has framed the Tea Party as potentially violent, [but] the Tea Party Movement and the Occupy movement [were] completely different. When we go to the Tea Party rallies, we leave the events spotless. They pay fees... and it's not violent, there's never been an arrest [at a] Tea Party movement here... certainly all the Kansas ones, they left things spotless because they thought that it was the right thing to do, but also the media was waiting for an incidence. Now with the Occupy movement, they would come and take parks... and hold property hostage. They would squat on it. They wouldn't pay fees and they stayed as long as they wanted. They tore up the places, there was violence, there was crime, there were rapes, murders, thefts, all kinds of stuff. So the Tea Party has made sure that they separate themselves from the violence. If they were like the Occupy movement — politically it would be bad for them. But the movement itself is not about physical violence. The threat, if there is any threat to government, it's being elected out of office, it's the people

who represent the Tea Party not putting their money into businesses or places that support these politicians that are doing things counter to the movement. The movement was never set up to be violent so it never seems to spiral towards violence. (Interview by the author, 13/11/13)

While the Tea Party perception of Occupy is bound to be biased, these observations do point to important differences in media strategy between the two groups. The Tea Party (perhaps partly because the members tend to be older – upwards of forty, often – and are usually Christian, and used to organising church and community events) were good at organising rallies. They were aware that the press was looking for stories, and so they made an effort to make sure that things like mess and violence were not there to be turned into stories against them. Occupy protestors, however, perhaps because of their self-identification with earlier 'hippy' movements, with their own ideas about self-governance and occupying space, were more vulnerable to a perception being constructed that they were 'dirty', 'hippy' and therefore anti-social.

The Tea Party members' utilisation of social media also helped their cause, especially in the beginning. The use of blogs meant that their ideas could be communicated without the traditional, mainstream media; speeches and interviews were put on YouTube and were received well, and the movement grew quite organically in a new form of word of mouth. The Internet meant that the movement could be grassroots but also widespread: "There would be no Tea Party movement had there not been a fundamental transformation of America's media landscape. The birth and growth of the grassroots, bottom-up Tea Party movement is a perfect example of how everyday citizens can use the new technologies to shape political events... The almost spontaneous organization of the Tea Party movement had as much to do with the nature and extent of the way the new media operates as it does with anything else" (Rasmussen and Schoen, 2010, 225-6). In this case, then, new media did change the game. But old media (and its own use of new media) would fight back.

The Tea Party movement, as it gained momentum and attention throughout the US, was picked up by Fox News and other mainstream broadcasters and media outlets. While this raised awareness of Tea Party issues and therefore helped recruitment and influence, it also provoked a backlash against the Tea Party from some media organisations. Paul Ibbetson of the Kansas Tea Party suggested concern among grassroots Tea Partiers that their local agendas had been largely misrepresented by the mainstream media. He said that the media had at first denied their existence, using the term 'astroturf' to describe the apparent falsity of their claim that they were a grassroots organisation. When in 2010, however, the Tea Party helped sway a lot of mid-term elections and Conservatives began to replace Democrats, the story changed again. As Ibbetson explained it:

> Then suddenly the Tea Party did exist! And it was a dangerous organization ready to start, you know, bringing back the KKK, lynching people, and hurting the poor, and all these evil things. And now, lately, with our... debate over spending... they say that the Tea Party has taken the Republican Party hostage. [So] now the TP's this giant power, like Dr Evil. (Interview by the author, 13/11/13)

While the Tea Party remained unpopular and was demonised by much of the media, however, it at least gained exposure and support from Fox News; Occupy had no comparable ally in the world of mass media. This association between the Tea Party and Fox News possibly came at a price, though. The Tea Party, which had started out being against corruption and the 'elite', found itself supported by the media organisation responsible for and connected to those businesses and individuals.

There was, therefore, division within the Tea Party movement as to their relationship with the Republican Party. Some were more comfortable than others about the implications of the close relationship between the Tea Party and individual Republicans (such as Sarah Palin), as well as with 'big business'. The Tea Party became divided between those who wanted to stay loyal to the original anti-corruption and anti-elitist ideas, and those who wanted to raise the profile of the Tea Party by compromising on these points and becoming closer to elements of the Republican Party.

Interestingly, both movements accuse the other movement of the same thing: while the Tea Party will argue that Occupy has infiltrated the Democratic Party (Rasmussen and Schoen, 2010, 22), those siding with Occupy will say that Tea Party ideals have changed the Republican Party politics. Perhaps there is truth to both 'criticisms' or observations; what is also true, though, is that these mainstream parties, originally the enemies of their populist counterparts, have usurped much of the movements, and it is unclear whether much real 'change' to the Republicans or Democrats is the consequence. The 'risk from above' was not only the threat of police repression; it was also the absorption of the populist movements back into the mainstream. It would seem that both Occupy and the Tea Party, in slightly different ways, have fallen victim to this.

Ultimately, both of these cases show interesting ways in which the authorities have undermined political movements, and importantly that these tactics change according to the particular characteristics or strengths of a group. Self-reflection and anticipation of these problems seem to be of high importance when planning not simply how a movement communicates to the wider public, but how it conducts itself at every level, for the smallest details (litter collection, for example) can have an effect on image and ultimate success. A group cannot be arrogant and expect that their vision will simply win everyone over, that the smallest of problems will not be depicted as catastrophes by the press, or that significant issues will be understood and forgiven. Optimism and vision may feel as though they will last forever, but unless they are accompanied by careful planning and *realpolitik*, they simply won't.

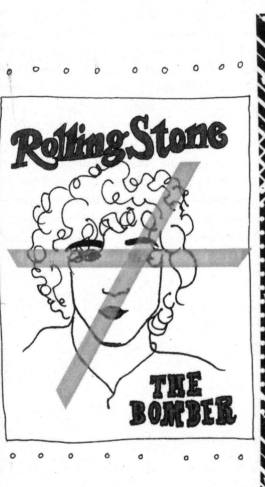

Chapter Seven

Narcissists with Bombs

The culture of PR and exhibitionism has lately given rise to a particularly narcissistic form of terrorism (the murder of Lee Rigby in Woolwich, and the Boston bombings, in 2012) and other political violence (the 2011 London Riots, for instance), in part because the media tend to focus on exhibitionist behaviour when they cover these stories, which means that we see more narcissism and less politics. The attention given to gratuitous violence in these instances has arguably inspired groups such as ISIS to produce a sustained campaign of sensationally gory propaganda in order to attract this attention for their own ends. While Michael Adebolajo (who murdered Lee Rigby) and the Boston Bombers' attacks were called 'amateurish', ISIS has used similarly excessive levels of violence but in a more methodical and sustained manner, with professional film-editing and the cunning planning of an advertising campaign. It is hard not to attribute some responsibility to news outlets in such instances where a group chooses a particularly violent PR method in response to the media's preferential treatment of it. As already mentioned, though, column inches and airtime do not necessarily correlate to political success. They are PR battles, violently fought, that do not win the war. And yet the tactic has remained popular for these individuals and groups.

Murder of Lee Rigby

The murder of Lee Rigby, for instance, was obviously designed with the media in mind. When Michael Adebolajo ran over and then decapitated soldier Lee Rigby with a meat cleaver, images of the attack quickly went viral on Facebook, Twitter, and YouTube, not to mention becoming a leading story for many days on the mainstream news media. As the *Guardian* pointed out, it was the "first UK murder to be transmitted 'live' on [the] Internet" (07/06/15). Adebolajo spent the moments after the attack talking to the press, in some attempt to justify or explain his actions, clearly aware of the inevitable media and then public interest:

> The only reason we have killed this man today is because Muslims are dying daily by British soldiers. And this British soldier is one... By Allah, we swear by the almighty Allah we will never stop fighting you until you leave us alone. So what if we want to live by the Sharia in Muslim lands? Why does that mean you must follow us and chase us and call us extremists and kill us? ... When you drop a bomb do you think it hits one person? Or rather your bomb wipes out a whole family? ... Through many passages in the Koran we must fight them as they fight us... I apologise that women had to witness this today but in our lands women have to see the same. You people will never be safe. Remove your governments, they don't care about you. You think David Cameron is gonna get caught in the street when we start busting our guns? Do you think politicians are going to die? No, it's going to be the average guy, like you and your children. So get rid of them. Tell them to bring our troops back... Leave our lands and you will live in peace. (From *Daily Telegraph* transcript: "Woolwich attack: the terrorist's rant," 22/05/13)

Clearly rehearsed, Adebolajo's speech nevertheless betrayed a sense of shock and nervousness in its speaker; the act and the narration did not quite fit. However pre-planned, the attack came across as nonsensical, even when its supposed point was explained for everyone to hear. The mainstream media described his speech as a "rant" (the *Daily Telegraph*), and despite Adebolajo trying to seem political and justified, his speech and actions were quickly dismissed as the ramblings of an evil madman. His stunt was quickly hijacked to become propaganda *for* the establishment rather than against it.

The particular focus on his being 'evil' via being a 'fanatic', 'ranting', etc. connected the threat of terrorism, as well as Islamic fundamentalism, to madness, lack of reason and sense, and individual chaos and insanity, thus discrediting the cause and its people. The headline "Muslim fanatic's evil rant after beheading" (the *Sun*), for example, connected 'Muslim', 'evil' and 'fanatic', implying a connection between Muslim identity and ideas, and 'evil' as well as 'mad'. So it conflated Muslim identity with this 'evil' existential threat. It also implied Adebolajo to be a monster, rather than a person, further adding to the idea that he was somehow sub-human. The use of the word 'barbaric', in particular, implied him to be uncivilised, mad and out of control (as well as 'other' and not 'British'). The *Daily Mail*'s headline, "Blood on his hands, hatred in his eyes," meanwhile, showed Adebolajo as guilty, violent and fuelled by emotion or madness, rather than any reason, which took away any sense of political agency in favour of an image of insanity and barbarism. The *Independent*, too, emphasised the idea of barbarism: "Unarmed. Attacked from behind. Butchered like a piece of meat" (30/11/13). The apparent treatment of Lee Rigby as a "piece of meat" made the perpetrator seem barbaric and monstrous rather than a political actor behaving strategically or with agency. The *Guardian* also referred to Adebolajo as "savage" (30/11/13), further characterising him as barbaric and sub-human.

In this context of demonisation, it seems unlikely that Adebolajo's pleas for the British public to throw out its government, to denounce the politicians, and so on, were taken remotely seriously by anyone. Rather, the murder of Lee Rigby became one more justification of surveillance and other tightened security measures against that public, who, rather than being inspired to rebel, or spurred to empathise with people in the Middle East, were further scared into support of, and subordination to, the British government.

Boston Bombings

The Boston Bombings were perpetrated by two brothers, Dzhokhar Tsarnev and Tamerlan Tsarnev, and from the moment they were identified, stories about their conflicting Chechen-American identities, their fall from innocence, and a certain 'good terrorist / bad terrorist' dynamic began to emerge. The press clearly favoured the younger brother, Dzhokhar, as did a niche group of teenage fans, who bemoaned on social media that he was too good looking to be so bad. *Rolling Stone* magazine ran with this idea, and used the 19 year-old bomber as its cover boy in a following issue, and fan-sites cropped up on the Internet (Segran, 04/03/15), mourning the jailing of a doomed, attractive teenager, as if he were a rock star.

This contributed to the idea that Dzhokhar was a weakened character with little political agency, rather than a politically powerful activist. There was an emphasis on the youth and naivety of Dzhokhar Tsarnaev – for example, the use of the word 'boyhood' by the *Arizona Daily Sun*; the mention of high school and the interviewing of high-school friends, such as in the *Anniston Star*: "'This is nothing we would ever expect': Friends of suspects shocked by allegations." This emphasis on youth demeaned the bombing suspects in the sense that they were seen as young, foolish and easily influenced. It also implied that Tamerlan Tsarnaev, the older brother and the second suspect, was a bad influence and that his brother, Dzhokhar Tsarnaev, was by comparison the impressionable innocent led astray (such as in the *Arkansas Democrat Gazette*: "Picture emerges of brothers on different paths: 1 had 'Terrorists' video file").

These bombings may have achieved some infamy for their perpetrators, but they were politically rather pointless and ineffective. As with the murder of Lee Rigby, the bombings served to frighten people, but the effect was not to switch sides and criticise the government, but to reaffirm solidarity and American identity, and to believe that the people, after all, needed the protection of their government. The 'terrorist threat' became 'real' again, even if the Boston attack had little to do with Al Qaeda or any specific revolutionary group.

The press used the attack to remind its readers of the 'evil' of this international terrorism and the 'enemy within', however. An emphasis on the innocent young American led astray by Islamic extremism emphasised that the American way of life was stronger and better than any other – especially 'Muslim' or 'terrorist' – way of life. That the suspects were American but also Chechen put a focus on ethnicity and the conflict between America and the 'other' – in this case the Muslim 'enemy within'. (The *Montgomery Advertiser*, for example, noted: "Botched escape: Chechen brothers kill 1 cop, wound another.") That there was apparently a personal conflict of Chechen 'other' vs. American underlined that conflict and difference. It also connected a domestic incident, without any obvious links to international terrorism, to a global threat and global conflicts, and therefore made this incident representative of a wider existential threat rather than a domestic problem.

Bostonians represented all Americans, and their ordeal became a crime against all of the US, rather than one city (giving a renewed sense of American identity, presumably). The lockdown was a communal 'nightmare', with a happy ending only thanks to the heroic police. Pictures of uniformed officers protecting the people and searching out their evil prey illustrated sensational stories of a terrified community and its innocent victims battling the forces of evil in the world.

The police were framed as 'good' protectors, therefore purging the community of evil and saving the people. They were at once tough and masculine (with guns, intimidating expressions and uniforms), and accessible and friendly (smiling and proud, and celebrated by the crowds). They were also shown to be victorious and successful in their mission to protect the people and carry out justice efficiently. The portrayal of the police using words like 'battle', 'gun battles' and other military language, despite a domestic setting, raised their importance and status, and the status of the drama, from domestic to international. Police officers were also seen as victims, occasionally, to emphasise their sacrifice for the community and their bravery in death. The use of the word 'slain' for example (in the *Daily Herald*) is quite romantic, and makes the death of a police officer seem like a form of martyrdom. This contributed to the 'unreality' of the story, and the transcendent goodness of the police.

The story was told in a generally (and typically) sensationalist manner, in fact, with emphasis on a huge chase, trapped civilians, and heroic police officers sweeping the drama to a cathartic close where Tamerlan Tsarnaev was killed and Dzhokhar Tsarnaev shot and caught. The events of the brothers' capture, incarceration and death were communicated with optimum drama; their demise was met with literal applause and widespread conviction that good had triumphed evil once again. Ultimately, the Boston Bombings, awful acts of violence, were politically ineffective, except as a way to remind Americans that they needed their government and police. It may have been a rebellion against the government, and its foreign policy, but it seems unlikely that the bombings did anything except act as publicity *for* the US government and its security services.

When it comes to PR, then, these cases (along with most overtly violent dissent) illustrate what not to do. Gratuitous violence may make a statement, and make the perpetrator infamous; it could fuel the perpetrator's own personal narrative of him or herself as a martyr and a soldier. But to the public, especially in a democratic society where other forms of dissent are allowed, it seems unnecessary and alienating, especially if the violence has no clear and obtainable political aims.

While longer campaigns of violence such as the Provisional IRA's Armed Struggle, and Hamas' campaign of violence against the IDF, worked better than the Boston Bombings and Lee Rigby's murder, this is because they were fighting against the state military for the most part, and there was a widely held belief (in their communities) in their legitimacy, and the state's provocation of organised, violent defence. Violence was one strategy among many. Even these long campaigns that involved violence have not achieved their main aims, however, and have alienated potential supporters of their causes, and it is arguable whether political violence of this kind ever really 'works', or –if it does – whether the negative effects of using violence (in PR terms especially) override potential strategic benefits.

In Erica Chenoweth and Maria J Stephen's 2011 study, *Why Civil Resistance Works*, for instance, their research shows that peaceful democratic dissenting movements are generally more successful than their more violent counterparts – more than twice as effective, in fact. From statistical analysis and case studies, the authors conclude that there are less obstacles to involvement for followers when a movement is non-violent, which gives those groups the edge (in terms of resilience, tactical innovation and general 'people power') when it comes to ultimately overthrowing a regime or fighting for democratic rights. Significantly, too, the authors found that non-violent initiatives were less likely to spiral into civil war and bloody counter measures – meaning that eventual success comes with less of a human price tag.

From a PR point of view, the use of violence undermines a movement because, if captured on camera, it becomes very easy for the media and establishment to portray that group in a negative way. That said, a movement can be overwhelmingly peaceful and receive the same treatment, either through association or provocation, or old-fashioned sabotage. There is a sense, perhaps, of 'damned if you do, damned if you don't', when it comes to dissenting movements and bad PR. Yes, violent campaigns receive negative PR. But so do peaceful movements. Nevertheless, a group would be wise to at least avoid a public image of being violent, and to manage the media as best it can even when confronted with unfair associations and portrayals. A dissenting movement should expect the media to be sensationalistic and biased; it should learn to deal with that reality, rather than be surprised when it all goes wrong. Subsequent chapters will outline ways of doing so, including the option of avoiding all publicity, in preference of other means of protest and subversion.

First, though, it is worth looking at the other extreme: the embracing of 'bad PR' by ISIS, and what this says about their relationship with the US and UK governments and the media, and what it means for other dissenting groups.

Chapter Eight

Shock and Awe: Performativity, Machismo and ISIS

The members of ISIS did not try to avoid a bad reputation. They did not give the impression of being a group willing to negotiate, or one that anyone would want to negotiate with. They did not give an image of being particularly reasonable or approachable. Rather, they communicated a visceral form of terror, a series of intimidating stunts and extreme acts of revenge. At the time of writing, it is really too early to tell what the effects of this political violence will ultimately be. But so far it is clear enough that 'public relations' is being used as a form of warfare in itself, rather than simply image-management.

Looking at the ISIS beheadings as a form of performed violence, we can understand these stunts as part of a media discourse between the US/UK and ISIS, as part of a related competition regarding ideas of masculinity and sexual superiority. By 'performed violence' (taking into account Juris' ideas about performativity in particular), it is understood that these beheadings are instances of violence in which their perpetrators communicate and "seek to produce social transformation by staging symbolic rituals of confrontation" (Juris, 2005). This understanding is in line with Jabri's understanding of violence as a means of political communication, resulting from its social and cultural context (Jabri, 1996), and Butler's ideas about performativity in relation to sexual identity, or gender as performed and communicated through violence, media and other means (Butler, 2009). Furthermore, the ISIS beheadings are part of a wider war of images (Mitchell, 2011), as well as a war of masculinities (Gentry and Sjoberg, 2007), and can be better understood as part of a tit-for-tat struggle between ISIS and the UK/US, using media to communicate competitive ideas of sexual superiority. By considering the ISIS beheadings through media and sexual discourse, their meaning and even cause – including the role of the US and UK in provoking such public political violence – can be better understood.

A War of Images

The ISIS beheadings of James Foley, Steven Sotloff, Alan Henning, David Haines and others were clearly intended to shock, and were intended as acts of revenge and deterrence regarding recent and planned US and allied foreign policy against the organisation. As ISIS communicated, through videos in which captives were made to recite monologues written by ISIS before being publicly beheaded, the killings were in response to Western foreign policy, and were communicated so that the people and leaders of those countries would be aware of the implications of further military action against ISIS.

> I am Alan Henning. Because of our parliament's decision to attack the Islamic State, I – as a member of the British public – will now pay the price for that decision. (Alan Henning, captive, speaking for ISIS; qtd. in Cobain et al, 04/10/14)

> You entered voluntarily into a coalition with the United States against the Islamic State, just as your predecessor Tony Blair did, following a trend amongst our British prime ministers

who can't find the courage to say no to the Americans. Unfortunately, it is we the British public that in the end will pay the price for our parliament's selfish decisions. (David Haines, captive, speaking for ISIS in A Message to the Allies of America; qtd. in Cobain et al, 04/10/14)

The blood of David Haines was on your hands, Cameron. Alan Henning will also be slaughtered, but his blood is on the hands of the British parliament. (Anonymous member of ISIS in *A Message to the Allies of America*; qtd. in Haberman, 13/09/14)

As well as specifically reacting to recent foreign policy against ISIS, these filmed beheadings were the latest assault in a "war of images" (Mitchell, 2011) between the US/UK, and their enemies in the War on Terror – originally Al Qaeda, and now ISIS. As Mitchell explained in *Cloning Terror: The War of Images, 9/11 to the Present* (2011), the US 'cloned terror' with its War on Terror, insofar as its efforts at counter-terrorism led to increased attacks and recruitment to terrorist organisations, parallel to a virtual 'cloning' of terror through the technological reproduction of images and other media depicting terror. Although Mitchell's insights are not concerned with ISIS, given that his book was published in 2011, his ideas are clearly relevant. It would seem that ISIS has simply fought back, in this 'war of images', by creating reciprocal propaganda videos and images that perpetuate terror, as well as committing terrorism in the physical sense through their continued combat and occupation of parts of Iraq and Syria. In the War on Terror, then, images are the arsenal and acquisitions of conflict as well as simply representations of more traditional, physical warfare.

This use of propaganda is rooted in a long-standing tactic of revolutionary groups – at times called 'propaganda of the deed' – in which violence and communication are merged to maximum effect. That tactic uses symbols (from religion or elsewhere) along with violence, and communicates a message with maximum exposure, emotional effect and resonance. In so doing, it has the potential to be extremely effective, as well as merely damaging.

What is interesting about ISIS's use of propaganda and violence, however, is not only that they have employed age-old tactics of propaganda and public violence in order to communicate a political message, but the context in which they have done so. One way of interpreting ISIS's use of filmed beheadings is as a reaction to previous similar methods of media and violence by the states they are fighting. Both the US and the UK governments and media have dehumanised and humiliated their enemies in the War on Terror through media as well as public violence, not to mention conventional warfare itself. An example of Western 'assaults' in the 'war of images' is the public humiliation of Saddam Hussein upon his capture in Iraq, with headlines such as: "Caught like a rat" (*Anchorage Daily News*, 15/12/03); "Saddam's long fall: Former ruler goes from ostentatious palaces to dirty holes in the ground" (*Anniston Star*, 15/12/03); and "Diligent hunters track down prey" (*Washington Times*, 15/12/03). These headlines were accompanied by pictures of Hussein looking disheveled, disorientated and in captivity – as well as his eventual death by public execution, as celebrated by the US especially. Osama bin Laden received similar treatment in the media, especially when he was killed, with headlines such as "U.S. forces gun down 9/11 mastermind" (*Daily Courier*, 02/05/11) and pictures emerging (although later confirmed to be fake) of a bloody corpse.

The photographs taken at Abu Ghraib, meanwhile, while not intentionally distributed by the government or military, nevertheless had a damaging effect when they were leaked, in that the pictures were aggravating not only to those in Al Qaeda and affiliated organisations, but also to the general (and particularly Muslim) public. They were not 'state propaganda' by any means, but their effect was still an assault comparable to other degrading and damaging images from the War on Terror.

A War of Masculinities

As well as currency in a 'war of images', these pictures and films signified assaults in another level of the conflict, a war of masculinities, as Sjoberg and Gentry put it (2007), whereby the US and its enemies (both Al Qaeda and now ISIS) compete with their ideas and manifestations of masculinity, to prove themselves more superior than the other.

> The relationship between the United States and Iraq had been framed as a competition between masculinities for more than a decade; each government told stories of emasculation of the other (Elshtain 1992b). Each government held standards of masculinity which the other did not meet. The United States relied on 'the contrast between the tough but tender and technologically sophisticated Western man and the hypermacho Arab villain from an inferior civilisation' (Niva 1998: 119) while the Iraqi government challenged the virility of this new, tender American masculinity. When masculinities compete, a hegemonic masculinity dominates subordinated masculinities. (Connell 1995) (Sjoberg and Gentry, 2007, 206)

This use of emasculation for the undermining of political power, on both sides, is part of a wider use of dehumanisation for that purpose. To reduce a person to something less than human, and to portray a person in sexual terms in order to dehumanise them, is a way to discredit not only an individual, but the cause and even civilisation that that person is seen to represent. The use of beheadings by ISIS can be interpreted, in this context, as a way of performing Iraqi ideals of masculinity (as tough, brave warriors), to contrast with and undermine those Western ideals of "tough but tender" (Niva, 1998, 119) and polite masculinity. By using such brutal and visceral methods of violence against Western men as the beheadings, ISIS asserted its masculinity as superior to Western masculinity, in order to express its supposed dominance in political and cultural terms more generally.

By considering ISIS's use of beheadings in the context of the 'war of images' as well as the 'war of masculinities', its showy, sensationalist violence can be understood as an effort to defeat the US and its allies in a propaganda war. By using gendered narratives of competing masculinities (through visceral, humiliating violence against Western men), and by communicating those narratives through film and other imagery (as well as the performed violence itself), ISIS's members are projecting an image of their organisation and their cause as superior to their Western enemies. In so doing, they are attempting to intimidate and dehumanise their enemy, as well as appealing to the people of those countries to put pressure on their leaders to abandon certain foreign policies (so communicating a more specific political message). The beheadings are at once a means of deterrence and revenge, and a simple assertion of dominance, using gendered narratives and performance.

So does this use of violent PR (to put it mildly) work? Having explored the meaning of ISIS's propaganda, it would seem that it 'works' in the sense that it is a counter-offensive against British and American media portrayals of prominent leaders such as Hussein and bin Laden, and a physical assault against Afghanistan and Iraq in particular. It 'works' in the sense that people have seen these videos and joined ISIS in Syria and Iraq. And it has worked in that these videos have intimidated people. But have they won the war? Or have they merely announced that it has begun?

I would argue the latter, though it is really too early to tell. Although far more planned and sophisticated than the Boston Bombings and murder of Lee Rigby, ISIS's public-relations offensive seems to share those characteristics of being intimidating but not necessarily indicative of any wider success. While ISIS may have recruited many people through their messages, they have probably alienated just as many, including people who may have been sympathetic to the cause without the gratuitous and sadistic violence. The problem with violence as communication, and communication as violence, is that while terror is effective at terrorising, it is not necessarily effective at much else.

As already mentioned, the communication of violence and terrorism in the media often reaffirms public support for Western governments (when it threatens those Western countries), rather than inspiring division within them. ISIS's PR campaign may have ultimately helped the British and American governments enlist support, both for stricter security measures domestically, and more conflict internationally. Crucially, this has a negative effect on other dissenting groups, because they then have to deal with these stricter laws and a less tolerant atmosphere as a result. So whether ISIS's version of public relations works in its favour or not, it certainly doesn't help other dissenting groups.

While a group like Occupy may not think that the workings of ISIS relate to its own struggle, since they certainly have little in common in the way of political ideas, it is foolish not to pay attention to the ways that a movement like ISIS can and does change the political landscape, and the way the public (and government) view all anti-establishment groups, no matter how different they are.

Chapter Nine

Clandestine Dissent

Given the problems with PR for dissenting groups, and the issues, especially, with public protest tactics such as marches and sit-ins, it is understandable that some groups shun publicity altogether, at least at the beginning of their political movement. As Chenoweth and Stephens (2011) point out, retreat can be as effective as action, and even a movement that does use public protest can benefit from occasions of withdrawal and contemplation. Mindless or un-thought-through marching about injustices or annoyances is unlikely to have much political effect at all. Being reactive at the expense of strategic is simply a waste of time. While marching and occupations may be cathartic and raise morale for a time, in the long run, if timed badly or not considered properly, they may do more damage than good. There is something to be said for discretion. Covert groups such as Anonymous and WikiLeaks, for instance, have arguably been more successful than groups that rely on protest in terms of affecting political change.

Anonymous

Anonymous presents a public image defined by secrecy – its members wear masks inspired by the graphic novel and film *V for Vendetta*, itself a story about Guy Fawkes and revolution. While Anonymous does organise public protests, these masks ensure anonymity for its members, and drive home their point that "we are many, they are few" – a united front rather than disparate, disorganised people, as other protests have a tendency to seem. It is their actions, though, that have given them renown, rather than more traditional publicity. The various groups and individuals who identify themselves as 'Anonymous' have hacked into big companies, institutions and even governments, such as PayPal, Visa, MasterCard, Sony, Tunisia, Israel, the Church of Scientology, the Westboro Baptist Church, and child pornography sites, among many others. Rather than a single group, Anonymous is more of an 'Internet gathering', decentralised and therefore harder to undermine, from a security perspective. While individuals have been arrested for specific crimes, the movement persists in part because of this structure. Problems have also arisen from that structural characteristic, however, including a lack of consistency and focus in the movement's aims, which has led to internal strife. For a sprawling, anarchic group, though, it has shown resilience: despite arrests, internal disagreement, and lack of a specific philosophy, Anonymous as a movement shows little sign of disappearing or even being undermined by state or corporate action against it.

WikiLeaks

WikiLeaks, while also a mainly anonymous movement that uses the Internet to affect political action that has also been described as hacktivist, differs from Anonymous in significant ways. Firstly, WikiLeaks does have leadership, and that leadership is not at all anonymous. Julian Assange, the Australian founder of the movement, is so well known and controversial that a film has been made about him. With infamy comes consequences, though; Assange at time of writing is still on house arrest in the Ecuadorian embassy and regularly appears in the press on the other side of the story.

WikiLeaks describes itself as a journalistic organisation, in that it publishes exposés such as news leaks and classified information from various (usually) anonymous sources. These leaks have become front-page stories many times, including a corruption investigation in Kenya, the *Collateral Murder* video, shot during a Baghdad airstrike in 2007, the Iraq War Logs, and classified documents relating to Guantanamo Bay inmates.

WikiLeaks differs from normal 'journalism', however, in that the emphasis is on the investigation – the finding out and divulging of secrets – rather than the writing up and the 'story'. Some describe WikiLeaks as a form of espionage rather than journalism (the US government, for example); perhaps it falls somewhere in between. The relationship of WikiLeaks to the press is an intriguing one, anyway. Famously falling out with the *Guardian*, whom they previously collaborated with to bring stories to light (or rather, to turn data into stories), WikiLeaks have had issues with the media, especially regarding differing practices and opinions regarding editing or editorial policy (or lack thereof). These disagreements have also occurred within WikiLeaks itself, notably sparking the departure of former German representative Daniel Domscheit-Berg in 2010.

WikiLeaks, despite its secrecy, has become something of a story itself, furthermore, and here it also has an interesting relationship with the press. While WikiLeaks describes itself as 'journalistic', its members are not journalists, but rather associates of them. They are the whistle-blowers and investigators, the enablers whose leads are then written up and articulated by the press. Nevertheless, WikiLeaks has changed journalism. It has also arguably endangered freedom of press in the sense that it has pushed the boundaries of 'legal' journalistic investigation to the point where it has broken laws over and over, and so this law-breaking clashes with the supposedly sacred 'right' of the press to its freedom. At the very least, the WikiLeaks exposés and controversies have raised questions about press freedom and what it means to have free speech that requires more defence and persuasion from the press and its supporters than ever.

Both Anonymous and Wikileaks have had the advantage of seeming legitimate to many people, as well as non-violent, even if some of their actions have been nevertheless illegal. The balance of illegal behaviour to perceived legitimacy is of course very important. While certain illegal action may be justified if it will be perceived as legitimate, it is a risky strategy. Snowden's leaking of the NSA intelligence, for example, while illegal, has been seen as a legitimate and justified act to many people, and he has been nominated for the Nobel Peace Prize because of this action. He has also been in exile for years now and faces life imprisonment for espionage if he returns to the US.

Anonymous, meanwhile, has operated as its name would suggest – covertly – but this hasn't prevented the authorities from findings and punishing several key operators, such as Jeremy Hammond, who pleaded guilty to violating the Computer Fraud and Abuse Act for being part of an attempt to break into the network of geopolitical analysis company Stratfor Global Intelligence Service. Mercedes Renee Haefer was arrested for being part of 'Paypal 14', which allegedly carried out a cyber-attack against PayPal, and Christopher Doyan is on the run after being arrested by the police in 2011 for attacks on Sony, PayPal, the Tunisian government, and the county website of Santa Cruz, California. If caught, he faces at least fifteen years in prison.

So, although these groups may have widespread support among the public depending on the action and the situation (some think of Chelsea Manning and Edward Snowden as heroic for standing up for American civil liberties, while others think of them as traitors, namely the government), the risks of lengthy jail terms still stand.

Illegal Internet activity such as WikiLeaks' use of illegal documents and Anonymous' hacking into government and commercial sites, therefore, can be effective for specific operations, but risks harsh punishment and repression. The risks need to be balanced against the gains, taking into account the likely perceived legitimacy of the action. 'Illegal non-violent' is generally a better image than 'illegal violent', however, and less likely to be termed 'terrorism'. This is always a good idea if a group wants to have any public support or perceived legitimacy, which is important no matter how obviously moral or righteous the cause seems to its own supporters. While it is perhaps good to have faith in one's cause, and to be loyal, it can be helpful to imagine things from the point of view of others, rather than dismissing them off the cuff. Most political movements probably think they are right and good; and yet every movement has its enemies and critics. While I am not suggesting that we should all pay attention to our critics unquestionably, it can be useful to understand why others may not agree with a specific set of ideas. Sometimes a simple reframing or explaining can bring in support and understanding. Other times of course the chasms can deepen. But paying attention to what makes a cause seem legitimate to people seems a sensible exercise for anyone whose success depends on a fickle public.

Chapter Ten

Turning the Camera

As we have seen in a number of cases, there are many ways that publicity can be a problem for dissenting groups, and many ways that well-intentioned (and not so well-intentioned) PR strategies can undermine them rather than support them. This is hardly exclusive to dissenting groups, though, even when they are up against a more powerful establishment. As we have touched on with regard to the Abu Ghraib scandal, as well as the exposés initiated by WikiLeaks, governments, media organisations and corporations are all vulnerable to bad publicity as well. In a democratic society, this is an important part of these institutions being kept in check. Freedom of press exists in part so that criticism of powerful institutions can be heard and debated, so that corruption can be exposed, and stories of public interest can reach that public.

In the US and the UK, there is a long history of the political exposé, from Watergate to Clinton. While there are probably far more cover-ups and silenced scandals than those reported on, the political effects of those stories that do make the headlines can be momentous. Briefly, we will look at some of these stories that have changed the political landscape, or at least ended careers, to get some idea as to the power of investigative journalism and the publicity of scandalous stories in the areas of government and international relations.

A History of Bad PR

Freedom of press and political scandal go hand in hand. But it is not just investigative journalism that creates these game-changing events where public awareness and perception of an issue are transformed. Sometimes images are leaked by ordinary people, or republished in such a way that a new audience sees them and they are given a new meaning, often also becoming the impetus for social change.

During the US Civil Rights movement in the 1960s, for example, the mother of David Jackson, a teenager lynched and burned to death, took photographs of his body in the casket, and held his funeral in Chicago (where more photographers were present) in order to publicise the atrocity of his murder. The transmission of this image emphasised David Jackson's humanity and his mother's pain, rather than allowing the sustained objectification and dehumanisation of him and lynching victims in general to continue. This was a watershed moment in the Civil Rights movement, where suddenly it became shameful to kill black people in such a brutal and racist manner, rather than a secret pride in white communities across the Southern states. The actions of David Jackson's mother were essentially to put across a counter-narrative, and to shame the perpetrators, "showing Jackson to be a person, grievable and victimized" (Apel & Smith, 2007, 64). The meaning of lynching pictures began to change – from being used as 'victory photographs' originally, compared to those taken after hunting or fishing – to being used as evidence to shame whole communities and their perpetrators during the Civil Rights era (Apel & Smith, 2007, 59).

This transformation of meaning and reception bears similarities with a more recent exposé: the Abu Ghraib scandal. Here, pictures of the degrading abuse of detainees in Abu

Ghraib prison, taken by military personnel for their own private collections, were leaked online, sparking outrage internationally and investigations into military abuse and torture. The images themselves were indeed shocking: a man in uniform, sitting on an Iraqi prisoner. Another pyramid of naked detainees, with a man and women behind them, smiling arm in arm, as if they are standing by a caught wild boar or large fish, or a well-organised barbeque. The moustached man (Charles Graner), again smiling and giving a thumbs-up sign, this time over a corpse, whose bloody eyes had been bandaged. A naked prisoner covering his ears, as several dogs bark at him, and soldiers watch on. Another prisoner chained to a bed-frame, with some underpants covering his face. These infamous scenes disturbed many people, and the perpetrators of the torture depicted were condemned by the relevant authorities. They transformed from clandestine mementos of hidden violence to evidence of serious crime. They went from being private victory shots to an international public relations disaster, and evidence of breaking of the Geneva Convention.

If there were any benefits of using torture in Abu Ghraib – and there is no evidence that there really were – then surely these were outweighed by the extensive damage to the reputation of the US and its sense of a moral high-ground, both domestically and internationally. Given that these acts were committed during a war where public image was so important – not only domestically, but in Afghanistan and Iraq, given the nature of the conflict – this was particularly problematic. In a battle for 'hearts and minds', these photographs were alienating and divisive, and extremely disrespectful. They communicated hatred and a complete lack of regard for the prisoners; they showed sadism and idiocy. The photographs, and the torture they revealed, showed the US to be immoral and deceptive, not heroic and compassionate as they would have surely preferred. This American war for hearts and minds took a significant blow when those pictures became a scoop.

Investigative journalism has also sought out such revelations and scandals. The Watergate exposé of the 1970s, for example, in which the Nixon administration tried to cover up a break-in at the Democratic National Committee in 1972, led to a US Congress investigation and further exposure of illegal activities undertaken by the Nixon administration. These included harassing activist groups and bugging political opponents, using the FBI, CIA and IRS to do so. Sixty-nine people were indicted, Nixon resigned, and the system was sent into disarray due to the widespread corruption, or rather, the discovery of it. Although it was a complex chain of events, much of the credit for that exposure can be given to the *Washington Post* reporters Bob Woodward and Carl Bernstein, as well as coverage in the *New York Times* and *Time* magazine. These press reports relied on anonymous whistle-blowers as well as original investigation on their part.

These days, the emergence of WikiLeaks means that the dynamic between whistle-blowers and investigative journalists is particularly interesting and complex, as discussed in the previous chapter. In these cases of 'bad PR' for a government or dominant community, political change comes from a critique of the establishment and its behaviour, rather than through organised dissent alone. It can support a movement, as the photographs of David Jackson did during the Civil Rights movement; or a scandal can work independently to undermine injustice and corruption, as in Watergate.

Perhaps it is no surprise, then, that investigative journalists are on government blacklists along with political activists. While much journalism aims, or says it aims, for 'objectivity', most journalism is political. Over the past few chapters, we have seen many examples of journalism that supports the establishment and governments' narratives about issues such as political violence, self-governance and protest itself. But some journalists, either in search of that elusive 'truth' and balance in their reporting, or because of more defined and specific political beliefs and motives, choose to cover stories and moments that have, implicitly, a spirit of dissent.

Investigative journalism can be a tool for a dissenting group, but it can also be an alternative to dissent; political critique is a way to be political without committing, necessarily, to one group or movement.

Photography and Dissent

Censored and uncensored, photographers and their publications have controlled how the American public regards battle. (MOELLER, 1989, 14)

When it comes to war and political violence, often images are the most hard-hitting form of 'news' to emerge from the front line, whether alongside words or not. The photography and films of photojournalists such as Don McCullen, Eddie Adams and Gilles Caron have provided images of distant and not-so-distant conflicts that often show another side to events framed in a certain way by the military and government. Eddie Adams' photograph of General Nguyen Ngoc Loan (the Republic of Vietnam's Chief of National Police) about to shoot a young Vietcong soldier, Nguyen Van Lém, became an anti-war icon, as did Nick Ut's (aka Huynh Cong Ut) 1972 photograph of a naked girl and other children running away from a napalm attack in South Vietnam. Don McCullen's image, 'Shell-shocked US Marine, Hue, Vietnam' (1968) shed light on the secret and psychological effects of war, while Gilles Caron's pictures of people on both sides of the Troubles in Northern Ireland showed a more human side to a 'story' that had been, as discussed earlier on, dominated by a particular 'terrorist' narrative, which forgot the many young people and ordinary civilians caught up in (and central to) the conflict (Anderson, 2013). While I have listed only a few iconic photographs and their makers, photographs of war and other forms of dissent are usually what the public sees first, and sometimes last, and these images shape their whole perception of war.

Most people in the West experience war vicariously, then, through the war photography that emerges from it (Mitchell, 2011, 1; Moeller, 1989, 7). The public and their ideas and opinions are changed by war photography, whether it is truthful and accurate or not. (While documentary photography may aim at objectivity, often, if not always, it betrays some subjectivity and point of view, which need not be seen as a problem.) War photography, in any case, is a mirror of the culture that produces it and reacts to it: "Rather than simple making culture, we also seem to be made by it" (Moeller, 1989, 4).

The consequences of these evolving opinions have significant implications for politics and business. While the images taken in World War II portrayed All-American Heroes saving their European allies, and those taken in Korea also presented that narrative – often with staged photographs (Sontag, 2003, 50) – by the time of Vietnam, with increased press freedom, public confusion about the point of the war in the first place, and protests at home fuelling public interest in the negative aspects of war, the narrative was far less positive. While the United States government has always attempted to show its forces, and its wars, as just and heroic, with Vietnam especially this story convinced less people, as a counter-narrative of the war as destructive and hopeless overrode the official line – a consequence, partly, of those photographs mentioned reaching so many people (Moeller, 1989, 5-6).

Dubbed 'the living-room war', the Vietnam War permeated American minds in an unprecedented manner, influencing culture and everyday life, as well as domestic politics, in an entirely new way (Sontag, 2003, 18). It also "exacerbated issues of race, poverty and gender. The negative emotions directed against the foreign enemy, which in previous wars had united the country, seemed during Vietnam to be turning inwards" (Moeller, 1989, 328). Politically, Vietnam made war unpopular with much of the American public, given the highly publicised deaths of soldiers as well as foreign civilians caught up in the conflict.

Images from the War on Terror have had similar effects to those from the Vietnam War on a contemporary public. The Abu Ghraib scandal, as well as more conventional war photography, has brought home the negative aspects of war to a wide and interested public. These images undermined support of the War on Terror, and perhaps even future wars, given the clarity with which it became apparent that the US and UK were fighting this 'terror' with their own version of it – despite other narratives of the US as an 'international policeman' and overall heroic force in the world, as had been the dominant narrative otherwise.

Photographs, then, whether 'leaked' from hidden sources, taken by a passing observer, or captured by a photojournalist, can change politics and undermine the official line. They can be used by dissenting movements to provide evidence for claims of injustice or crime, or they can be communicated through the more mainstream press, managing to cut through other narratives of war and protest. They can be explicitly or implicitly a form and means of dissent.

Art and Dissent

If photography, film and written journalism can change the world, then what about art? Often regarded as rather superfluous and disconnected from the world of politics and protest, art is nevertheless used in many political situations to express ideas and personal experiences. Some even say that art has a responsibility to bear witness to atrocity, to shed light on human suffering and injustice (e.g. Tolstoy, 1897). Picasso's *Guernica* (1937), for instance, told of the bombing of Guernica during the Spanish Civil War by Italian and German planes, in collaboration with Spanish Nationalists, bringing global attention to the atrocity. Before that, Goya created a series of prints, *The Disasters of War*, (1810-20), protesting the Dos de Mayo Uprising of 1808 and the Peninsular War of 1808-14. These have become iconic anti-war images, as well as personal accounts and works of art.

More recently than Goya and Picasso, artists such as John Keane, George Gittoes, Ben Quilty and Anita Glesta have responded earnestly to the wars in Bosnia, Iraq, Afghanistan, and Rwanda, as well as events connected to the War on Terror such as 9/11 and the Abu Ghraib scandal. John Keane's work has drawn inspiration from trips to Central America, Northern Ireland and the Middle East, including a stint as an official war artist appointed by the Imperial War Museum. His work, primarily painting, often depicts violent subject matter, but he clarifies that sensationalism is nevertheless to be avoided: "I don't think [visual art] should be sensationalist, but at the same time it shouldn't flinch from addressing those sort of difficult questions" (Interview by the author, October 2014). He also helps explain the relationship between art and politics and propaganda, stating that even if art is influenced by personal perspectives and feelings about one's subject, it should avoid becoming propaganda:

> Art should be the reverse [of propaganda]; it should be revelation. If an artist has a propagandist agenda, then that is to the detriment, I think, of the art, in that ideally, art should be about revelation not concealment. But inevitably you do have a viewpoint, you do from observations take sides, and that inevitably comes through... [But] if a polemic takes over, then the art suffers. (Interview by the author, October 2014)

It is clearly a fine line to be aware of, then: that between art *about* politics, and political art. While Keane is clear that he avoids being too drawn-in by any 'polemic', other artists, such as George Gittoes, consider it their duty to take a side (anti-war) and to create work that is a form of activism. Having made films as well as drawings and paintings in numerous warzones, including Iraq, Afghanistan, Bosnia, Rwanda, Somalia, South Africa and Southern Lebanon, Gittoes depicts the gruesome brutality and atrocity of war in his work, unflinchingly. *Rwanda Maconde* (1995), for example, details a massacre at the Kibeho refugee camp, and includes drawings of a mother and child in a mass grave, and a boy staring into space, traumatised. *Night Visions* (2010), meanwhile, depicts United States soldiers and their experiences in a fictionalised war zone, based on Gittoes' own experiences of Iraq and Afghanistan during the recent War on Terror. His body of work is expansive and varied, but the subject of political violence and war persists throughout, and his anti-war sentiments remain consistent. He does not think his depictions are sensationalist or use violence gratuitously though, and sees his work as a tonic to mass media and particularly Hollywood depictions of war:

> I cannot think of any example in my art where I have used violence gratuitously. It has only ever been depicted as a means to either alert the world to atrocities or to make an important point. (Interview by the author, December 2012)

Gittoes also considers artists as in a privileged position to be duty-bound to understand aspects of war and humanity, where other forms of media cannot.

> The great thing about art is that regardless of how the state may try to control its distribution, the artists themselves have unlimited freedom to explore what it is to be human… When I hear news reports of the ongoing conflict in Mali and Syria and see the new atrocities every night… I want to be there as I feel I can contribute my lifetime of experience to assisting the people there, and to bring a different kind of message about what is happening to the world. (Interview by the author, December 2012)

Gittoes is firmly of the belief that art can be (and should be) a form of dissent. He considers his own work to be an extension of his humanitarian and activist work, and says that his film-making and painting are ways of communicating the horrors of war to a wider audience, particularly in a world where mass media exhibits its own political bias, and is thus complicit in focusing on some issues more than others. While Gittoes' form of activism would not suit all causes or groups, it is an interesting idea to consider. Art is an area of communication often thought to be beyond the realm of political communication, and perhaps it's all the more effective for that dismissal. As Ben Quilty (also a painter) said recently in an interview (with the author), artists are often given freedoms that journalists are not, because in certain situations, at least, they are considered less of a threat (Spens, 2014a). In many ways, artists are less threatening than investigative journalists. But if one sees the function of protest as recording injustice and discontentment in the face of atrocity, then art, broadly understood, is a particularly good way of documenting dissenting ideas and observations. And while it may not be as directly challenging as investigative journalism or incriminating photographs, it is nevertheless not only a valuable form and means of dissent, but also a way to understand injustice, political hypocrisy and crime more generally, and so is important simply in that sense, and is complementary to dissent and critique.

Aside from what tends to be known as 'fine art', of course, there is the use of art for dissent in a more direct or propagandistic sense. During the Troubles, murals became a way for people to express their ideas and feelings of injustice, on both sides. Images would change with political events; they would commemorate fallen heroes and protest oppression and injustice (and often, a mixture of the two). In a conflict about land, public space and political-social identity, the murals became an important way for people to assert themselves and their own. Free Derry Corner, for example (a side of a building with the famous slogan "You Are Now Entering Free Derry"), became iconic, and remains to this day a means of remembering those involved in the conflict as well as the dreams they pursued. Recently in Palestine (and elsewhere), Banksy (and many others) have used murals and graffiti similarly, to protest and record. The world over, in nearly every dissent situation, people paint murals, slogans and tags in the name of their cause and their comrades.

On a smaller scale, but just as effectively, posters have also carried the ideas and outcries of many protesters. From the 'votes for women' campaigns of the early 20th century, to anti-apartheid marches of the 1960s, and from climate change awareness to the Parisian Situationist posters of the 1950s and 1960s, movements have had their slogans and recognisable images, their collages and satire, within the easily reproducible frames of protest posters (Spens, 2014b). Graphic and linguistic techniques and tricks vary slightly from movement to movement, but the means remains reliable and popular, whether these images are seen by the naked eye, reproduced in traditional print, or posted on social media.

On a smaller scale again (physically), those with an artistic bent have lent their skills to satirical cartoons. A long tradition, caricature has captured the absurdities, hypocrisies and idiocies of establishment and anti-establishment groups alike. Whether *Punch* mocking the IRA during the Troubles or the Suffragettes during the fight for women's rights, or the staff of *Charlie Hebdo* satirising Islamic fundamentalists and well-known politicians, cartoonists have been on a front line of their own (the staff of *Charlie Hebdo*, sadly, in a literal sense). There is, in fact, a long history of cartoonists in particular being punished brutally for their drawings. Ilan Danjoux compiled a list of artists who were silenced (or had serious attempts made to do so), including:

the torture of an... artist named Pauson, for his attack
on Greek leadership, described by both Aristotle and
Aristophanes; Honore Daumier, a French artist, imprisoned
for his lampooning of King Louise Philippe and his court;
English cartoonist David Low, placed on the Gestapo's
extermination list; Naji Ali, assassinated in 1987 for his
criticism of Arab and Palestinian leaders; in 1998, the Kurdish
cartoonist Dogan Guzal criticised his government as weak,
and was subsequently sentenced to 16 months in a high-
security prison; and, [before their infamous assassinations],
the Charlie Hebdo team had been targeted before. In 2011 after
the publication of an issue that billed the Prophet Muhammad
as a "guest editor", their officers were gutted by a fire bomb.
(Danjoux, 2007)

As Larsen points out: "A newspaper is undeniably a weapon of
war, and its power can be measured against the efforts taken
to disarm them" (Larsen, 2015). As fellow cartoonist MATT
pointed out, though – in a cartoon featuring some masked,
heavily armed assassins outside the *Charlie Hebdo* offices saying to each other "Careful, they might have pens" (14/06/15)
– that revenge killing of cartoonists seemed absurdly unfair,
however powerful or provocative they might be.

Literature and Dissent

Whether through satire or poetry, literature is also a way
to record and witness political violence, and especially
the personal and communal experiences of such conflict.
From the perspectives of bystanders as well as those actually involved, literature can question and interrogate the
human tendency to fight and commit atrocities, as well as
exploring the common experience of enduring them. Novels

such as Hemingway's *The Sun Also Rises*, and poems such as Longley's *The Ice Cream Man* and *Ceasefire* provide insights into the wider experience of dissent, as do Remarque's *All Quiet on the Western Front* and Kevin Powers' *The Yellow Birds*. Heller's *Catch-22* and Vonnegut's *Slaughterhouse 5* take darkly satirical perspectives, while Camus' *The Rebel* and Kafka's *The Trial* and *The Penal Colony* expose the absurdities of war and dissent.

Some literature even inspires dissent through politically conscious ideas and sympathies, such as Shelley's *Masque of Anarchy*, which was written in reaction to the Peterloo Massacre of 1819, and went on to inspire various dissenting groups. Yeats' one-act play (written with Lady Gregory in 1902), *Cathleen ni Hoolihan*, meanwhile, was written about the 1798 rebellion and the play's namesake, the symbol of Irish Nationalism, Cathleen. As a character in the play, she requests nothing less than a blood sacrifice for her cause (Irish Nationalism), declaring of those who fight for her: "They shall be remembered forever, They shall be alive forever, They shall be speaking forever, The people shall hear them forever." These words and ideas were woven into the fabric of modern Nationalist mythology. Three poets – Patrick Pierce, Joseph Plunkett and Joseph MacDonagh – were also executed following the Easter Rising on 1916, and Bobby Sands, himself a poet, famously died as the result of hunger strike. Poets such as Longley and Heaney, meanwhile, took the role of the observer and were less overtly political.

Music and Dissent

In Northern Ireland, given the tradition of Irish ballads, rebel songs such as *The Fields of Athen Rye*, *Come Out You Black and Tans*, *The Wearing of the Green* and *The Wind That Shakes the*

Barley not only added to the mythology of the cause, but also served to raise morale and bring people together in a more direct, instant way. Bands such as Wolf Tone and Dubliners these days follow the tradition of writing ballads about massacres, making folk heroes of Republicans; sometimes ballads could be poetical, other times less so, but they are rousing and political all the same.

On the other side, Loyalist bands have long been used not only to intimidate during marches and bring others together, but also to encourage very young people, sometimes children, to become politically involved through playing flute or drums in the bands. Reacting to the Republicans, they have songs such as: *Follow, Follow the Billy Boys*, *Daddy's Uniform*, *Father's Advice* and *The Sash My Father Wore*.

Beyond Northern Ireland, dissent and music have a long history, particularly when it comes to anti-war protest songs such as (famously) Bob Dylan's *Masters of War*, The Specials' *Free Nelson Mandela*, U2's *Bloody Sunday*, Billie Holliday's *Strange Fruit*, The Sex Pistols' *Anarchy in the UK* and Serge Gainsbourg's controversial *Le Marsellaise*.

The list, of course, goes on and on. Music, with literature and art, is often one of the most effective ways to bring people together in a political movement, whether or not it becomes that movement's 'public image' *per se*. The BBC News is unlikely to play a soundtrack of *The Sash My Father Wore* when it reports on a bombing attempt in Belfast, and the US government is hardly likely to give a selection of opinions and feelings on its latest foreign policy that includes *Masters of War*, however popular or accomplished. Art, music and literature, while sometimes used by the government and mainstream media to tell the story of one movement or another, tends not to until that phase is history, and something to recall national pride (for instance when reprinting and recording war poetry on the anniversary of D-Day). Art tends to remain on the fringes of political critique and dissent, even though often it is art that captures the nuances and atmosphere of a time and movement the best. That said, it is worth remembering that protest is not only about effecting political change in the present; it is also about recording a time, and people's opinions. It's about reminding future generations that there might have been another way, and perhaps there still can be. It's about sparking debate, inspiring ideas and bringing people together. Art, literature and music, then, are in the midst of that always. Stories, written, sung and painted, can not only provide counter-narratives, but can help us understand dissent from every side. Songs, posters, cartoons and poems can be calls to arms, and expressions of peacefulness alike.

Although seeming too 'Romantic' can be used against individuals and their political movements, that spirit is nevertheless alive and need not be extinguished. Being aware of public relations and the current political landscape does not mean abandoning Romanticism in the wider sense – rebellion, passion and innovation are needed now as ever. The Romantics gave validity to the emotions and experiences of many individuals, rather than abstract notions of reason and logic; they encouraged new ways of thinking and seeing the world. Those alternative perspectives are still relevant today, and the general attitude of open-mindedness and innovation can enable still new ideas and solutions to our current problems. Although the image of that movement and its legacy might not help win over the newspapers, the substance behind it may do. We have much to learn from the Romantics – poets and revolutionaries alike.

Thou art Justice – ne'er for gold
May thy righteous laws be sold
As laws are in England
Shield'st alike both high and low.

(PERCY BYSSHE SHELLEY, 1819)

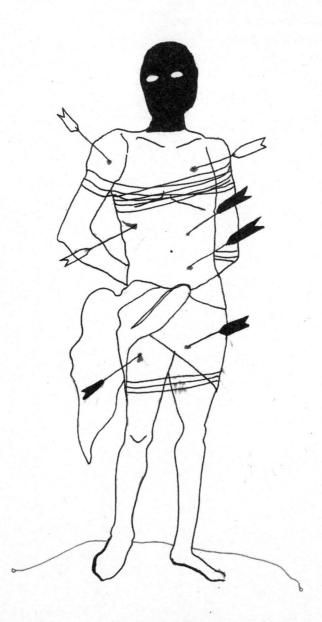

Chapter Eleven
Beyond Martyrs and Terrorists

Having contemplated a wide range of dissenting groups, from violent to peaceful and from publicity-hungry to clandestine, several important points have emerged which can give us some idea as to how public relations can help and undermine groups whose ideas challenge the status quo. While a study of ISIS, for example, may not at first seem relevant to a group such as Occupy or Stop the War, given their significant differences on almost every level as movements, we have seen in fact that there are pertinent lessons to be learnt. The way in which ISIS has used social media and film could inspire the most peaceful group, and the way in which it has alienated people with violence could dissuade other groups from accepting such behaviour. That said, the fact that ISIS's opportunistic sadism has attracted not only recruits but also an audience suggests a voyeurism (at least) in many people, which can help us understand why the media covers some stories as if they are action movies, and not others.

The main findings that have emerged from the cases covered are: (a) Violence and other illegal behaviour often gets publicity, but usually doesn't help the cause, and is unsustainable long-term; (b) Non-violent civil resistance has been shown to be more effective than violent, but it can be hard to get publicity, so must be managed well; (c) While the Internet can be useful for some groups, it is best seen as one tool of several, and it is necessary to understand the risks involved in over-reliance on the Internet; (d) Often investigative journalism (particularly in association with groups such as WikiLeaks) is the most effective means of dissent, where the public relations is focused on the political problems themselves rather than individuals and a group's image. Art, music and literature, furthermore, are often overlooked but have proven uniquely valuable over the years as means of dissent as well as means of more detached (or philosophical) critique and contemplation about the issues dissenting groups are concerned with.

Of course different groups will have particular PR strategies, depending on their various principles and aims, but the ideas that emerged from a broad discussion on dissent and the media should give us an understanding of the ways in which groups are successful, or less so. The murder of Lee Rigby for example, showed what not to do if one wants to be taken seriously. Elements of the Tea Party movement's strategy, however, along with successful populist groups such as Stop the War and Occupy, show the specific measures that have worked to their benefit, which can therefore be applied elsewhere. Covert measures as used by WikiLeaks and Anonymous, meanwhile, have worked in the short term, but have provoked great repression from above because they involved illegal action, which may even have had a negative effect on other dissenting groups (although, conversely, their findings have inspired many to fight for civil liberties and be aware of state repression and surveillance).

Overall, dissenting groups run the risk of being depicted (almost by default) as reckless, extreme, and impulsive or irrational, to varying degrees, according to their behaviour but also an existing stereotype of dissent as illegitimate and possessing 'Romantic' qualities (at best), and criminal, threatening qualities (at worst). A public who are treated as a docile audience rather than politically powerful participants in a democracy seem to justify this presentation of political actors as mere pantomime villains, and the running of society as a spectacle. If that is to change then it is that public who must demand it and engage with politics seriously, as well as political actors who can encourage and lead them in doing so.

The Future of Dissent

So what can be done to redefine dissent, and utilise the democratic right to protest, in a culture where the trivialisation of dissent can sell stories and weaken anti-establishment political thought? The ideas that emerged from this discussion suggest that when handling the media, first of all, careful risk management is key, especially with regard to publicity. A clear and long-term PR strategy and plan to manage the media makes sense, including: other tactics aside from demonstrations and an over-reliance on publicity; avoidance of violence, and disassociation with violent factions, as this is not good publicity in the long term; and infiltrating or influencing the media where possible, to define the narrative. Propaganda goes both ways after all.

Dissenting groups can of course use the media to their advantage through telling the public of their grievances, repression and injustices, which will support the cause and likely increase its popularity and acceptance. While the established media may have no interest in representing dissenting groups accurately or sympathetically, meanwhile, local media may do, as well as counter-culture publications and art more generally. A movement that is embraced by its own community, whether local, cultural or political, is likely to be more sustainable than one that is not.

It also helps to know what (and whom) you are up against, to be intelligent about spotting infiltrators and predicting repression. Police and other spies regularly infiltrate non-violent and violent groups; this should not be a shock, but an expectation, or a risk to be managed. By knowing legal rights, having legal representation on hand, and keeping good relations with the authorities where possible, a dissenting group has a far better chance of affecting political change, and being sustainable.

It is important, furthermore, to remember that dissent, when legal, is a democratic right, not a crime. An asserted effort must be made to sustain that democratic right, in the face of reforms that may effectively criminalise these democratic rights. This is perhaps the most important point: if a group's aims are democratic in essence, then the awareness of undemocratic reforms and punishments is key. Any democratically orientated dissenting group should campaign against undemocratic reforms even if it is not its main political focus, for its own sustainability and legal right to function. The main threat to dissent is undemocratic criminalisation of that dissent.

Dissent can, however, adapt to even undemocratic and unfair repression, and repression can alienate the people that the (UK and US) governments depend on for power. The question for these governments is whether they want their own people to become 'the enemy within', or whether it's a better idea to compromise with their demands, when democratically presented. This is why going the non-violent, legal route is best for dissenting groups in the long term; it is the best shot at true change, with the eventual support of the population, community and ultimately the government that is meant to represent them.

It would be ideal to move into a world beyond PR, where substance matters more than rhetoric, and where people are not so easily swayed by tabloid tales of heroes and villains and a political system that often resembles a pantomime. Must we accept a world where people seem to respond to this political circus, rather than reason alone? In a world where people are taken in by stories of villains and heroes, rather than facts and good arguments – should dissenting groups communicate their political points accordingly? While it may be overly idealistic, on this point I would suggest the greatest change. Rather than simply seeking to control the narrative in which one plays a part, as the next section will explain, it makes sense (I think) to change the way the narrative is told. Only then can we hope to move beyond the usual clichés of political theatre.

Changing the Narrative

One of the main ways in which art, literature, music and journalism work is by changing the narrative of the cause and people it explores as its subject, as we have seen in various cases so far. Bobby Sands, for instance, through self-sacrifice, changed the story of the Troubles, and public perception of his cause. Many others have taken the path of self-sacrifice (or 'martyrdom', depending on a religious influence), to convince others that they and their cause are the victims rather than the 'bad guys' or guilty party in any given conflict. Since the political spectacle tends to dismiss most ambiguity in favour of simple binaries of 'good' and 'evil', 'winner' and 'loser', it makes sense that some dissenters, frustrated by perceived misunderstanding of their specific situations, would engineer a stunt whereby they place themselves in the 'good' role – in these cases by emphasising their victimhood, endurance, and, sometimes, creating a story of strength and ultimate death that recalls stories of the Saints and other religious and mythological figures.

In South Vietnam in the 1960s, a group of Buddhist monks set themselves on fire (separately) to protest the persecution of Buddhists under the rule of the Roman Catholic government led by President Ngô Đình Diệm. Self-immolation, in this context, was part of a long religious tradition as well as being a tactic of political dissent. "Non-violence is more than a strategy in this tradition; it is a way of life that respects all life" (Fierke, 2013, 161). More recently, in Tunisia in 2010, 27 year-old Mohamed Bouazizi set himself on fire in the country's capital, Tunis, to protest maltreatment by the Tunisian authorities. The event sparked the Tunisian revolution and the wider Arab Spring.

In the case of Bobby Sands, martyrdom served as a foil to the 'terrorism' narrative that had thus far dominated public perception of Irish Republicanism. In other cases, however, such as Palestinian suicide bombers, the use of the idea of martyrdom can fuel the terrorist narrative. The main difference is that with Sands (and other individuals who died for their cause) only the dissenter(s) died; with suicide bombers, many uninvolved others die too. In the case of Sands, he was guilty of very little, and any damage seemed to be directed at himself. He came across as symbolising the tortured and the victimised. While suicide bombers also play this role, it is combined with other techniques and roles, to change their narrative in another way. The suicide bomber brings many other people down with him or her.

Suicide bombing serves a tactical role as well as a symbolic one, furthermore: if a group doesn't have drones or other high-tech weaponry, then a human 'bomb' can facilitate that focused attack, without depending on money or technology. An individual carrying explosives can target a specific place or person with relative ease. Symbolically, too, a suicide bombing projects an image of fearlessness and ultimate self-sacrifice along with, obviously, terror. In the context of the Israel-Palestine conflict, suicide bombers recalled religious ideas about personal honour and redeeming oneself through martyrdom, as well as solving a tactical issue of wanting to target specific places and people without the necessary equipment. Hamas delivered the message that their group, their people, would sacrifice anything, and were thus braver than the Israelis on account of self-sacrifice. It also made them a formidable enemy; with suicide bombers, they posed a grave and adaptable threat.

Al Qaeda followed Hamas in this use of suicide bombing, and the conflict between Western armies and the 'terrorist' Al Qaeda also became a 'war of masculinities', as discussed previously with reference to ISIS. In the case of Al Qaeda, the implication of using suicide bombers was that their group and people represented a more fearless, ruthless form of masculinity, compared to the Western type. In short, Al Qaeda communicated through suicide bombing (and other ruthless forms of violence) that they were bigger and braver, more masculine than the West.

In these cases of political violence, symbolic warfare and physical aggression were combined in the use of suicide bombing, to change a narrative (from losing, ill-equipped groups, to fearless, determined threats to the West). Sands, previously, along with nine other young men, used the hunger strike to undermine the story of his cause being terrorist, and transformed the story and cause's image in that way.

But claiming martyrdom (with or without other victims)

isn't the only way to change the narrative. While making one-self look like the 'good' victim or the fearless military threat has proven effective in the cases mentioned (usually in situations where religious identity is important), making the other side look 'bad' works just as well, and usually with less victims – which seems far more sensible to me, not only in the sense that violence alienates people no matter how aggrieved a side feels, but also because it seems a grave waste of life and potential to throw people into the firing line for the sake of sending a message, however important that message is. If a group is aggrieved, then committing heinous acts of violence, whether against the self or not, seems merely to muddy the waters and make peace and reconciliation extremely difficult, if not impossible for a long time.

Often exposing atrocity is far more powerful than wreaking vengeance anyway: Abu Ghraib, for instance, was such a scandal because it showed the apparently 'good' America acting sadistically and inhumanely. Merely avenging crime simply brings your own side down to the level of the perpetrator – as the US was seen to do by allowing torture of prisoners during the War on Terror. To fight terror with terror seems absurd, after all.

In order to challenge the propaganda surrounding the British Army, and specifically its recruitment drive targeted at teenagers and even children, Veterans for Peace UK made films (*Action Man: Battlefield Casualties*) that showed, with some dark humour, the real impact of war on soldiers and veterans, rather than the state-sponsored bravado and glorification of conflict. The 'action men' in the films include "PTSD Action Man... with thousand-yard stare action" and "Dead Action Man... coffin sold separately." "Paralysed Action Man" has legs that "really don't work" (Gilmour, 2015).

More subtly, novels such as Kevin Powers' *The Yellow Birds* provide a more nuanced account of war that exposes not simply 'good' and 'bad' but the complex combinations and moral difficulties associated with, in this case, serving in the War on Terror. Similarly, though from an earlier time, Hemingway's *Fiesta: The Sun Also Rises* speaks of the disenchantment and numb despair that followed the Second World War for the so-called 'lost generation'.

These novels are not really what we would think of as 'public relations'. And yet when it comes to the public understanding something as complex but oft-simplified as war, as 'good' and 'evil', as injustice and despair – well of course it takes a few hundred pages of empathetic prose to communicate any genuine message about the reality of these situations. And that, ultimately, is what is required if people are really to relate to one another. If the aim of public relations, in the sphere of politics or elsewhere, is to communicate messages and ideas and emotions to the public, then a group or individual must do more than stand in a space, shouting (or blowing themselves up), waiting for other people to tell their story or explain their actions. They must tell their stories themselves. They must explain their experiences, their ideas, their injustice – and perhaps not only through the most obvious channels and using the most clichéd tropes.

There have been a lot of martyrs for a lot of stories about 'good' and 'evil' in the press about politics. I'm sure Nietzsche would have a lot to say about that merry-go-round of saints and sinners and their respective wills to power; that this sort of slave morality is reprehensible and ultimately weak, perhaps. That rather than spin between binaries in reaction to one another, it may be better to become somewhat free-spirited (Nietzsche, 1886), or the 'sovereign individual'

(Nietzsche, 1887). I won't go into a spiel about Nietzsche here, but I do think that there is something to be said for bucking the trend, those roles of 'good' and 'evil', and being more imaginative and free in our discussions of what it is to be an individual in society, and how we relate to and participate in politics.

This book has been a series of contemplations rather than a prescriptive text, which is all that really makes sense when different dissenting groups have such varying situations and demands; I cannot hope (and do not wish) to provide a comprehensive guide to protest PR, as such. However, if I may take a moment here as this book concludes to have some point of reflection, I would like to be a little on the libertarian side of things, to take that idea of the 'free spirit' and 'sovereign individual', and adapt it to my own times and dilemmas. Should I wish to be subversive, I would do so by stepping back, stepping away, and taking time to think before acting. I would focus on keeping our civil liberties protected from passing state interests, sparked by fear of elusive 'baddies'. I would retreat and think and then tell the stories that seem important. I would support those who write them.

Perhaps the essence of this book, then, comes down to a rather simple message after all: a wish to tell stories of substance rather than perform re-runs of a clichéd pantomime show, where political actors play simply the villain or martyr. A hope that we can see beyond horror shows and shock tactics and keep a clear head. A wish to explain things properly, and to appeal to reason and emotion at once; to change the narrative from one of excessive simplicity and emotional manipulation to one of common sense and intelligence. Have slogans, by all means, but do not end the conversation there.

Dissent, then, even if its ideals are Romantic and revolutionary, and even if the individuals involved are too, should be careful not to let those ideals dominate the image of the movement in a negative way, and to be aware that certain tactics, while reminiscent of rebellions past, are not practical for a group intending to affect real political change in the existing political climate. Self-control, planning and intelligence are more important. As Shelley wrote:

> *Blood for blood – and wrong for wrong –*
> *Do not thus when ye are strong.*
> *With folded arms and steady eyes,*
> *And little fear, and less surprise,*
> *Look upon them as they slay,*
> *Till their rage has died away.*

If we pay attention to the Romantics, we can see that they had more to offer than battle cries, aesthetic violence and heroic failure. They also promoted peaceful civil resistance, integrity, open-mindedness, persistence and humility. It is these aspects of their ideals and work that we would do well to remember, and to publicise.

Bibliography

Anderson, D. (2008): "Bobby Sands, Hunger, and How to Make a Nation Disappear," in *3:AM Magazine*, 12/11/08. Accessed on 08/06/15 at: http://www.3ammagazine.com/3am/bobby-sands-hunger-and-how-to-make-a-nation-disappear/

—— . (2013): "Picturing Derry: Review," in *Studio International*, 17/07/13. Accessed on 12/06/2015 at: http://www.studiointernational.com/index.php/picturing-derry

Apel and Smith (2007): *Lynching Photographs*. Berkeley and Los Angeles: University of California Press, Ltd.

Armey, D., and Kibbe, M. (2010): *Give Us Liberty: A Tea Party Manifesto*. NY: HarperCollins.

Barber, T., and Boldrick, S. (eds.) (2013): *Art Under Attack: Histories of British Iconoclasm*. London: Tate Publishing.

Bolt, N. (2012): *The Violent Image: Insurgent Propaganda and the New Revolutionaries*. London: Hurst & Company.

Bowcott, Owen (2010): "The legacy of the Bloody Sunday killings," in the *Guardian*, 15/06/10. Accessed on 09/06/15 at: http://www.theguardian.com/uk/2010/jun/15/legacy-bloody-sunday-killings

Butler, J. (2009): *Frames of War*. London: Verso Books.

—— . (2009): *Performativity, Precarity and Sexual Politics*. AIBR. Revista de Antropología Iberoamericana. Vol. 4, No. 3 (Sep-Dec 2009), pp i-xiii. Madrid: Antropólogos Iberoamericanos en Red. Accessed on 01/12/13 at: http://www.aibr.org/antropologia/04v03/criticos/040301b.pdf

Carr, M. (2011): *The Infernal Machines: An Alternative History of Terrorism*. London: Hurst & Company.

Chenoweth, E. and Stephens, M. J. (2011): *Why Civil Resistance Works*. NY: Columbia University Press.

Chomsky, N. (2002): *Media Control: The Spectacular Achievements of Propaganda*. USA: Seven Stories Press.

Chomsky, N. (2012): *Occupy*. London: Penguin Books.

Cobain, Laville and Jalabi: "Isis video shows murder of British hostage Alan Henning," in the *Guardian*, 4/10/14. Accessed on 25/10/14 at: http://www.theguardian.com/uk-news/2014/oct/03/alan-henning-isis-syria-video-murder

Connell, R. W. (1995): *Masculinities*. Berkeley, California: University of California Press.

Danjoux, I. (2007): "Reconsidering the Decline of the Editorial Cartoon," in *PS: Political Science and Politics*, Vol. 40, No. 2 (April 2007), pp. 245-8. The American Political Science Association.

De Quincy, T. (1827): "On Murder Considered as One of the Fine Arts," in *Blackwood's Magazine*. Accessed on 01/09/15 at: https://www.gutenberg.org/ebooks/10708

Dobson, C. and Payne, R. (1977): *The Carlos Complex: A Study in Terror*. Great Britain: Hodder & Stoughton.

Edelman, M. (1988): *Constructing the Political Spectacle*. Chicago: The University of Chicago Press.

English, R. (2003): *The Armed Struggle*. Oxford: Oxford University Press.

—— . (2009): *Terrorism: How to Respond*. Oxford: Oxford University Press.

Elshtain, J. B. (1992b): "Just War as Politics: What the Gulf War Told Us About Contemporary American Life," in D.E. Decosse (ed.), *But Was It Just? Reflections on the Morality of the Persian Gulf War*. New York: Doubleday.

Fierke, K. M. (2014): *Political Self-Sacrifice: Agency, Body and Emotion in International Relations*. Cambridge: Cambridge University Press.

Formisano, R. P. (2012): *The Tea Party: A Brief History*. USA: The John Hopkins University Press.

Gell, A. (1998): *Art and Agency: An Anthropological Theory*. Oxford: Oxford University Press.

Gentry and Sjoberg (2007): *Mothers, Monsters, Whores: Women's Violence in Global Politics*. London and New York: Zed Books.

Gilmour, C. (2015): "War Veterans Make Some Dark Films to Protest the British Army's Recruitment of Child Soldiers," in *Vice Magazine*. Accessed on 23/06/15 at: http://www.vice.com/en_uk/read/action-man-battlefield-casualties-ptsed-soldiers-348

Greene, J. (2011): "The Media's Dirty War on Occupy," in *Solidarity US*. Accessed on 10/06/15 at: https://solidarity-us.org/node/3639

Greenslade, R. (2011): "The IRA hunger strike and Fleet Street's graveyard of truth," in the *Guardian*, 17/06/11. Accessed on 21/06/15 at: http://www.theguardian.com/commentisfree/2011/jun/17/ira-hunger-strike-fleet-street

Haberman, Z. (2014): "David Haines video: Full transcript of ISIS footage that allegedly depicts beheading of British aid worker," *New York Daily News*, 13/09/14. Accessed on 25/10/14 at: http://www.nydailynews.com/news/world/transcript-isis-video-alleged-beheading-david-haines-article-1.1938691

Halliday, J. (2013): "Woolwich attack first UK murder to be transmitted 'live' on internet," in the *Guardian*, 19/12/13. Accessed on 07/06/2015 at: http://www.theguardian.com/uk-news/2013/dec/19/woolwich-attack-first-uk-murder-transmitted-live-internet

Hermann, P. (2011): "'Occupy' memo could discourage victims from reporting assaults," in the *Baltimore Sun*. Accessed on 10/06/15 at: http://www.baltimoresun.com/news/maryland/baltimore-city/bs-md-ci-occupy-baltimore-rape-20111019-story.html#page=1

Hoffman, B. (1998): *Inside Terrorism*. London: The Orion Publishing Group.

Horn, H. (2011): "How the World is Covering Occupy Wall Street" in the *Atlantic*, 14/10/11. Accessed on 10/06/15 at: http://www.theatlantic.com/international/archive/2011/10/how-world-media-is-covering-occupy-wall-street/246677/

Jabri, V. (1996): *Discourses on Violence: Conflict Analysis Reconsidered*. Manchester: Manchester University Press.

Juergensmeyer, M. (2000): *Terror in the Mind of God: The Global Rise of Religious Violence*. Berkeley and Los Angeles: University of California Press.

Juris, J. S. (2005): "Violence Performed and Imagined: Militant

Action, the Black Bloc and the Mass Media in Genoa," in *Critique of Anthropology*. New York: Sage Publications.

King, P. (2011): on CNN, 17/11/11. Accessed on 01/09/15 at: http://edition.cnn.com/videos/

Larsen, J. (2015): "A Cultural History of Satirical Cartoons and Censorship," in *JSTOR Daily*. Accessed on 14/06/15 at: http://daily.jstor.org/cultural-history-satirical-cartoons-censorship/

Lehr, P. (2013): "Still Blind in the Right Eye? A Comparison of German Responses to Political Violence from the Extreme Left and the Extreme Right," in Taylor, Currie and Holbrook, eds., *Extreme Right-Wing Political Violence and Terrorism*. New York: Bloomsbury.

Lewis, J. quoted in the *Baltimore Sun* (2011): "[the statement] in no way discourages people to contact the police," 19/10/2011. Accessed on 10/06/15 at: http://www.baltimoresun.com/news/maryland/baltimore-city/bs-md-ci-occupy-baltimore-rape-20111019-story.html#page=1

Livingston, S. (1994): *The Terrorism Spectacle*. Boulder, Colorado: Westview Press.

MATT, for the *Telegraph*, reprinted in: "How illustrators responded to the Charlie Hebdo attack in Paris," by Rob Alderton in *It's Nice That*. Accessed on 14/06/15 at: http://www.itsnicethat.com/articles/je-suis-charlie-responses

Meisel, S. (2006): "State of Emergency," in *Vogue Italia*, September 2006. Italy: Condé Nast. Accessed on 08/08/13 at: http://www.theage.com.au/news/fashion/designer-terrorporn-now-in-vogue/2006/10/26/1161749253595.html

Milmo, C. (2014): "Revealed: How MI5 watched the wrong Oxbridge academics – Christopher Hill and Eric Hobsbawm," in the *Independent*, 24/10/14. Accessed on 08/06/15 at: http://www.independent.co.uk/news/people/revealed-how-mi5-watched-the-wrong-marxist-oxbridge-academics--christopher-hill-and-eric-hobsbawn-9814170.html

Mitchell, W. J. T. (2011): *Cloning Terror: The War of Images, 9/11 to the Present*. Chicago and London: The University of Chicago Press.

Moeller, S. D. (1989): *Shooting War*. New York: Basic Books Inc.

Morgenstern, M. (2011): "Female Protester Raped at Philadelphia Camp, Suspect in Custody," in the *Blaze*. Accessed on 10/06/15 at: http://www.theblaze.com/stories/2011/11/13/female-protester-raped-at-occupy-philadelphia-camp-suspect-in-custody/

Moseley, R. (1985): *Thatcher Urges War on Terror: Voluntary Coverage Ban by Media Proposed*. Chicago: The Chicago Tribune.

Mulder, S. (2015): quoted in *RT.com*, 26/03/15. Accessed on 21/06/15 at: http://rt.com/news/244141-isis-artifact-destruction-propaganda/

Nietzsche, F. (1886): Beyond Good and Evil.

—— . (1887): The Genealogy of Morals.

Niva, S. (1998): "Tough and Tender: New World Order Masculinity and the Gulf War," in M. Zalewski and J. Parpart (eds.), *The 'Man' Question in International Relations*, Boulder, CO: Westview Press, p.119.

Ogilvie et al. (2004): *George W. Bush Deliver us from Evil: The Effects of Mortality Salience and Reminders of 9/11 on Support for President*. Sage Publications.

Plate and Tuohy. (1993): "Los Angeles Times Interview: John Major – Even Under Fire, Britain's Prime Minister Holds His Own," in the *Los Angeles Times*, 20/06/93.

Ramsay, G. (2015): *Jihadi Culture on the World Wide Web*. London: Bloomsbury.

Rasmussen, S., and Schoen, D. (2010): *Mad as Hell: How the Tea Party Movement Is Fundamentally Remaking Our Two-Party System*. NY: HarperCollins.

Rosenthal, L. and Trist, C. (2012): *Steep: The Precipitous Rise of the Tea Party*. Berkeley and London: The University of California Press.

Schultz, J. (1998): *Reviving the Fourth Estate*. Cambridge: Cambridge University Press.

Segran, E. (2015): "These 3 Women Are The Accused Boston Bomber's Biggest Fans," in *Refinery* 29, 04/03/15. Accessed on 07/06/2015 at: http://www.refinery29.com/2015/03/80705/boston-bomber-dzhokhar-tsarnaev-fans

Sontag, S. (2003): *Regarding the Pain of Others*. London: Penguin Books.

Spens, C. (2014a): Interview with Ben Quilty in *Studio International* on 04/07/14. Accessed on 13/06/15 at: http://www. studiointernational.com/index.php//ben-quilty-interview

——— . (2014b): "A World to Win: Posters of Protest and Revolution," in *Studio International*. Accessed on 13/06/15 at: http://www. studiointernational.com/index.php/world-to-win-posters-protest-revolution-review-mcmanus-dundee-v-a

Taylor, A., Gessen, K., and the editors from *n+1*, *Dissent*, *Triple Canopy* and *The New Inquiry* (eds.) (2011): *Occupy! Scenes from Occupied America*, London and New York: Verso.

Taylor, Currie & Holbrook, 2013 (eds.) (2013): *Extreme Right-Wing Political Violence and Terrorism*. UK: Bloomsbury.

Terrorism Act (2006). Accessed on 06/08/15 at: http://www. legislation.gov.uk/ukpga/2006/11/section/2

Todorov, T (2009): *Torture and the War on Terror*. UK: Seagull Books.

Wilde, O. (2009 (1890)): *The Picture of Dorian Gray*. Fairfield, Iowa: World Library.

Wilkinson, P. (1992): "International Terrorism: New Risks to World Order," in John Baylis and Nick Rengger (eds.), *Dilemmas of World Politics: International Issues in a Changing World*, pp. 228-9. London: Clarenden Press.

Wordsworth, W. (1999 (1888)): *The Complete Poetical Works*. London: Macmillan and Co. Reprinted by *Bartleby.com*. Accessed on 10/02/14 at: http://www.bartleby.com/145/ww285. html

Wyant, C. (2012): "Covering the Coverage: What's behind the media's depiction of Occupy protesters?" in Mint Press News, 23/02/12. Accessed on 10/06/15 at: http://www.mintpressnews. com/covering-the-coverage-whats-behind-the-medias-depiction-of-occupy-protesters/20980/ y

Acknowledgments

Thank you to those in the International Relations department at the University of St. Andrews, especially Richard English, Orla Lynch, Alex Danchev, Gilbert Ramsay, Roddy Brett, Peter Lehr, Karin Fierke, Sally Cummings, Caron Gentry and Tim Wilson, for their encouragement, advice and words of wisdom on matters of dissent and rebellion. Thanks to *Tooting Free Press*, who published an essay on dissent and romanticism that started this book; to *E-International Relations*, who first published an essay on ISIS, parts of which have also found its way into this book; and to *Studio International*, who published my interviews with artists Ben Quilty, John Keane and George Gittoes. Thanks to Charlie Gilmour and Heathcote Ruthven for discussion, inspiration and friendship. Thanks to Carrie Kania, for writing advice and support in the beginning.

Thank you most of all to Darran Anderson, a true collaborator, for love and support and our beautiful baby Caspian (and for holding him when I had a paragraph to finish).

And of course thank you to Tariq Goddard and everyone at Repeater Books, for publishing this book and providing a haven for subversion and spirit.

Repeater Books

is dedicated to the creation of a new reality. The landscape of twenty-first-century arts and letters is faded and inert, riven by fashionable cynicism, egotistical self-reference and a nostalgia for the recent past. Repeater intends to add its voice to those movements that wish to enter history and assert control over its currents, gathering together scattered and isolated voices with those who have already called for an escape from Capitalist Realism. Our desire is to publish in every sphere and genre, combining vigorous dissent and a pragmatic willingness to succeed where messianic abstraction and quiescent co-option have stalled: abstention is not an option: we are alive and we don't agree.